THE LAST DAYS OF THE TITANIC

Fr. Frank Browne SJ, MC
Chaplain to Irish Guards, 1915–1920

The Last Days of the
TITANIC

PHOTOGRAPHS AND MEMENTOS
OF THE TRAGIC MAIDEN VOYAGE

E. E. O'DONNELL SJ

Foreword by
Dr. Robert D. Ballard

Roberts Rinehart Publishers

DEDICATION
To Those who Died that Night.

International Standard Book Number 1-57098-201-5

Library of Congress Catalog Number 97-69059

Published in the United States and Canada by
Roberts Rinehart Publishers
6309 Monarch Park Place
Niwot, Colorado 80503

Distributed to the trade by Publishers Group West

First Published in 1997 by
Wolfhound Press,
68 Mountjoy Square, Dublin 1

Reprinted 1997, 1998

10 9 8 7 6 5

Book and cover design by Ted & Ursula O'Brien
Photographic prints by Davison & Associates, Dublin
Duotone separations by Colour Repro Limited, Dublin
Typeset by ArtLine Limited
Printed and bound in Belgium by Proost N.V.

Cover Photographs:
Front: Captain Smith looking down from the starboard bridge wing of *Titanic* at Queenstown
Back: A White Star letter. (Both photographs from The Father Browne SJ Collection)

CONTENTS

Founder/President
Edward S. Kamuda

The Titanic Commutator
The quarterly magazine of the
Titanic Historical Society
continuous publication since 1963

Editor-in-Chief
Edward Kamuda

Publisher
Karen Kamuda

Historian
Donald Lynch

Reference
Ray Lepien
Ken Marschall
Eric Sauder

Business Staff
Anne Gorman
Barbara Kamuda

The
Titanic Historical Society
Collection
The Titanic Museum
in Indian Orchard
The collection is an educational, yet poignant experience about the *Titanic* with rare documents next to more familiar pieces -- a third-class menu; a wool carpet piece cut from a first-class stateroom on C-Deck; a wood fragment from a lifeboat; boarding passes for the *Titanic*; postcards and letters mailed from the ill-fated liner; the *Marconigram* ice warning from S S *Amerika; Titanic* lookout Frederick Fleet's rendition of the fatal iceberg; an original *Titanic* blueprint presented by the builders, Harland and Wolff and recently discovered plans for a 1,000' four-funneled liner. An entire section on *Titanic*'s sisters *Olympic* and *Britannic*, photographs, china, posters, newspapers, books, original paintings, sheet music, survivor keepsakes and association pieces are at this unique site.

Marine Museum at Fall River
Half of the THS Collection is here including Mrs. Astor's lifejacket, Lookout Fred Fleet's discharge book and a deckchair retrieved by the *Minia.* Be sure to see the 28' 1-ton *Titanic* created for the 1953 20th-Century Fox production, *Titanic.* The THS was entirely responsible for bringing the film model to the museum in 1985.

THE TITANIC HISTORICAL SOCIETY, INC.
PO Box 51053 - Henry's Building, 208 Main Street
Indian Orchard, Massachusetts 01151-0053 USA
Mon.- Sat. 10 - 4 closed Sun./holidays   Phone (413) 543-4770   Fax (413) 583-3633

12 September, 1996

Father Eddie O'Donnell S.J.
Gonzaga College
Sandford Road
Dublin 6
Ireland

Dear Father Eddie,

We were so pleased to learn the news of your new book, "Father Browne's *Titanic*." If you recall when you kindly addressed our Titanic Historical Society convention in Belfast, No. Ireland at the Europa Hotel last April, you mentioned your plans to publish his photographs and diary.

My wife, Karen, our historian, Don Lynch, and myself are quite excited about this project and it is an honor as officers of the T.H.S. to be of assistance. These images by Father Browne are of immense importance to *Titanic* historians as well as the general public who have developed an intense curiosity about this great liner owing to increasing publicity. In her brief existence there are very few actual illustrations to chronicle not only the vessel but also those who were aboard *Titanic*'s historic voyage. Few will be able to read this book and not come away without a greater understanding of the people pursuing daily shipboard activities and the beauty and grace of the vessel herself. Some of the passengers and crew in the photos were saved while others shared a different fate. Among the survivors was young Douglas Spedden who can be seen on deck spinning a whip top while others watch his performance. Not so fortunate was Captain Smith, viewed in another photograph, looking down from the bridge at the tenders below at Queenstown. From that height he observed passengers boarding the ship as Father Browne departed and *Titanic* sailed into her destiny.

These remarkable and haunting images are a treasure and we are grateful to Father Browne for leaving a legacy of memories in the photographs of the ship that has become a legend. Likewise, to yourself, our deep appreciation for presenting this document for future generations.

Yours sincerely,

Edward S. Kamuda

Edward S. Kamuda
Founder/President
Titanic Historical Society, Inc.

FOREWORD

By Dr. Robert D. Ballard

I felt privileged when Father Eddie O'Donnell came to visit with me at my home on Cape Cod in January 1997. In a certain sense, I felt he was a kindred spirit as I was aware that he had made a major discovery in 1985, when he found Father Browne's collection of more than 42,000 photographs. I knew that ten books of these pictures had already been published, including one in French. The purpose of his visit was also clear and I was delighted to oblige him by agreeing to write this foreword.

Some of Father Browne's *Titanic* photographs were already familiar to me since I had used many of them in my own books (such as *The Discovery of the Titanic*) but I had not seen the album in its entirety, nor had I read Frank Browne's account of the maiden voyage as far as Queenstown.

Looking through these photographs taken 85 years ago recalled very vividly to me my first glimpses of the liner on the sea floor in 1985. The one of the lifeboat hanging in its now empty davits and the one of the anchor being raised for the last time were poignant reminders of what we found two-and-one-half miles beneath the surface of the Atlantic Ocean.

Let me single out one picture in particular. During my second visit to the liner in 1986, as our underwater robot, *Jason Junior,* slowly passed by the gymnasium windows, remnants of the gym equipment could be seen, including some of the metal grillwork that had protected such contraptions as the electric camel – a turn-of-the-century exercise machine. Frank Browne's photograph of the interior of that gymnasium and the card given to him by Mr McCawley – the ship's physical education officer – bring home to me in a really tangible way the fact that human beings once exercised their muscles here. The single word 'Lost' in Frank Browne's caption reinforces my belief in the sacredness of the gravesite.

Apart from the photographs I was fascinated – as I am sure every reader will be – by Frank Browne's description of his days on board; and I was intrigued by the poem he wrote afterwards. The additional materials that have been included make this a most unusual book; so it is with great pleasure that I commend Father O'Donnell's work and wish the book the success it deserves.

One of Frank Browne's last photographs of Titanic, *taken at Queenstown (Cobh) on 11 April, 1912. He sent this picture to the Odell family and it is sometimes erroneously attributed to them. The twelve photographs taken by the Odells, who disembarked with Frank Browne at Queenstown, are the only other surviving pictures of* Titanic *taken by maiden voyagers.*

Acknowledgments

My sincerest thanks to those who have helped me put this book together: Father John Guiney SJ of the Jesuit Generalate in Rome (who kept the Browne album safe for many years); Karen Kamuda of Ludlow, Mass. (who masterminded my profitable journey to New England early in 1997); her husband Ed Kamuda (who not only wrote the Preface but showed me around his Titanic Museum at Indian Orchard, Mass. and gave me many fascinating souvenirs); Dr. Robert D. Ballard of Woods Hole, Cape Cod (who kindly invited me to his home and agreed to write the Foreword); the editor of *The Belvederian* (for permission to reproduce the article given in chapter five); Andrea & Eddie Doherty of Long Island (for their hospitality in New York and for showing me White Star relics there); Mr. Tom McCusker, Administration Manager of Harland & Wolff Ltd. (for inviting me to the liner's birthplace in Belfast); Mr. Donald Hyslop of the Maritime Museum, Southampton (for showing me the *Titanic* memorabilia there); Melvin Lash and Jasper Coffman of the Marine Museum, Fall River, Mass. (for showing me their 30-foot model of the *Titanic* and many other treasures related to the liner); Donald Lynch and Ken Marschall of Redondo Beach, California (for invaluable help with the captions); Stephen Brooks, Military History Officer, Portsmouth City Museum; Lt. Cdr. Liam Smith of Cobh (who formerly worked for James Scott & Co., the shipping-agents who sent Frank Browne his *Titanic* ticket); David Aherne, the 87-year-old former pilot of Cobh (who is blessed with a brilliant memory and gave me its full benefit); Vincent McMahon, Manager of Irish Ferries, Cork (who went to a lot of trouble in producing documents invaluable to my research); Dr. Pat Donlon and the staff at the National Library of Ireland (for constant services rendered); Maura Kennedy of the Gilbert Library, Dublin (for letting me read the Dublin newspapers of April, 1912); Edwin Davison of Dublin (for computerising Father Browne's captions and finding the relevant ones for this book); his father, David Davison, Head of the Photographic Department, Dublin Institute of Technology (for making the prints and for his enlargement of the final photograph of Captain Edward Smith); Ursula and Ted O'Brien (who did such a fine job in presenting my material); and to Seamus Cashman of Wolfhound Press.

Gonzaga College,
Dublin 6,
Ireland.

INTRODUCTION

My purpose in this introduction is threefold. First I want to tell the reader who is not familiar with the life and work of Father Browne a little about that heroic life and that remarkable work. Secondly, I will try to tighten the focus and situate this *Titanic* album in the context of Father Browne's photographic output as a whole. Finally I want to zoom in still closer in order to give an understanding of the importance in Frank Browne's life of ships and shipping and to explain how, from his earliest years, he developed an interest in maritime and nautical matters which would endure throughout his life.

Life and Work

Sunday's Well is a leafy and prosperous suburb of the city of Cork, terraced high above the River Lee as it makes its two-armed embrace of Munster's capital on the south coast of Ireland. It was there in 1880 that Frank Browne was born on 3rd January. He was the eighth child of Brigid and James Browne and he was baptised in the Cathedral Church of SS. Mary and Anne, Shandon – which stands beside the famous steeple of that name – on the 8th day of January. The following day his mother died of puerperal fever.

Brigid Browne had been the eldest daughter of James Hegarty, Lord Mayor of Cork. Like her husband James, a wealthy merchant, she had grown up in Sunday's Well and had been prominent in the social and charitable activities of the local parish. James, too, was to meet a tragic end:

he drowned while ocean swimming at Crosshaven, County Cork, when Frank was in his teens. As a result, the father figure in Frank's life was his uncle, Robert Browne, the Bishop of Cloyne whose cathedral stood above the town of Cobh. At that time Cobh was known to Irish emigrants and other transatlantic passengers by the name of Queenstown.

Frank Browne's schooldays were spent at the Bower Convent in Athlone, Christian Brothers College in Cork, Belvedere College in Dublin and Castleknock College in County Dublin. He graduated from the last of these in 1897 and then set out on a tour of mainland Europe with his brother and his new camera – a gift from Uncle Robert. The photographs he took in France, Italy and Switzerland were the first shots in a salvo of photography that is still reverberating a century later.

On his return to Ireland in September 1897, Frank entered the Jesuit novitiate at Tullabeg and duly took his first vows of poverty, chastity and obedience two years later. He then went up to the Royal University in Dublin where he was a strict contemporary of the not-so-strict James Joyce. Since both of these young men had been to Belvedere College, they would have known one another quite well. Indeed 'Mr Browne, the Jesuit' was to make several appearances, many years later, in *Finnegans Wake*. In their Honours BA examination in 1902, Joyce scored 313 out of 900 in English; Browne scored 352. In Latin Joyce received 352 (out of a possible 1,200) as against

Browne's 815. In different senses, they were both late developers.

In 1902, Frank was sent to study philosophy for three years at Chieri, near Turin in the north of Italy. We know that during his summer holidays he made a serious study of painting, going to see the Old Masters in the galleries of Milan, Florence and Venice as well as those in nearby Turin and Genoa. What he learned from these Italian masterpieces, in such matters as balance, compositional skill and attention to detail, would be of immense importance later in his own artistic medium.

Returning to Dublin in 1906, Frank Browne was sent to teach in his old alma mater, Belvedere College. During the first of the five years he taught there, he founded *The Belvederian* as a college journal, and the Camera Club to which he invited many distinguished lecturers. This period of a Jesuit's formation is known as 'Regency' and was designed to give experience of work at the chalk-face of secondary education to which most Jesuits at that time returned after ordination.

In 1911 Frank crossed to the south side of Dublin's River Liffey to begin his theological studies at Milltown Park. So it was during his second year there that his Uncle Robert gave him a treat: a trip of a lifetime – a two-day cruise on the world's largest liner, RMS *Titanic.*

Frank's liner voyage brought him from Southampton to Cherbourg and from there to Queenstown where he disembarked. We shall be examining these days in more detail later. Suffice it to say here that it was not his only brush with death.

Frank Browne was ordained to the priesthood by his Uncle Robert on 31st July, 1915 and his first assignment was as chaplain to the Irish Guards who were then serving on the front lines in France and Flanders. For the duration of World War I, he devoted himself to the troops and earned a reputation for his heroic dedication to his duties. He was injured five times, on one occasion needing to have his jaw wired back into place. His lungs were severely damaged by mustard gas in April 1918.

His commanding officer, Colonel (later Field Marshal Lord) Alexander, described Father Browne as 'the bravest man I ever met'; he knew that the chaplain earned the MC and Bar from the British authorities, the French *Croix de Guerre* and his personal decoration by the King of the Belgians.

Among the treasured possessions of the Irish Guards at their headquarters in Wellington Barracks, London, is a leather-bound album of Browne's photographs entitled 'The Watch on the Rhine'. These were taken during 1919 when the guardsmen were stationed in Cologne and Bonn. The chaplain was not demobilised until the Spring of 1920 when he returned to Dublin. The War of Independence was then raging in Ireland. On the eve of Kevin Barry's execution Father Browne cycled to the Viceregal Lodge in the Phoenix Park to plead for the life of his former pupil in Belvedere. The Viceroy, Lord French (who had led the British Expeditionary Force to war in 1914), refused to intervene.

Not long afterwards, the ex-chaplain was appointed Superior of St. Francis Xavier's Church in Dublin, but his health began to deteriorate gradually. His lungs were still contaminated by the 1918 gassing. When other remedies failed, his doctor recommended an ocean voyage and a warmer climate. This was how Father Browne came to spend two years in Australia where he was soon well enough to photograph the horse-races in Melbourne, the yacht-races in Sydney Harbour, cricket matches in Adelaide and Brisbane, and a sheep-shearing competition at Kangaroobie.

On his way to Australia he had stopped off at Cape Town and taken many interesting pictures of the Cape Province of South Africa; he returned via Ceylon (now Sri Lanka), Aden, Suez, Salonika, Naples, Toulon, Gibraltar, Algeciras and Lisbon, thus adding an important international dimension to his collection of photographs.

From 1925 to 1929 Father Browne was back at his post in Dublin and then he became a member of the Retreats and Missions staff of the Irish Jesuits, a position which he held for the rest of his life. This work brought him as a preacher to practically every parish in Ireland and to many churches in England, Scotland and Wales. He worked mainly in the evenings, so he had the daylight hours at his disposal for photographing the neighbourhood, its beauty spots and its ugly sights, its people old and young.

In 1927 Browne became a vice-president of the first Irish International Salon of Photography. The two other vice-presidents were Chief Justice Hanna and General Eoin O'Duffy, Commissioner of the Irish police. The president was Sir John Lavery RA and the Salon was such a success that it continued every other year, under the same officers, until the outbreak of World War II in 1939.

During the 1930s the Jesuit was commissioned to do photographic work by several Irish government departments, by the governing body of the Church of England and by the British Museum. He contributed illustrated articles to many periodicals, including *The Kodak Magazine*. He became a personal friend of the Managing Director of Kodak Great Britain, George Davison, who was in a position to give the priest free film for the rest of his life.

That life continued until 1960. Lord Alexander travelled from England to visit Father Browne on his deathbed in Dublin and Lord Nugent wrote his obituary in *The Irish Guards Association Journal* where he said that 'everyone in the Battalion, officer or man, Catholic or Protestant, loved and respected Father Browne and he had a great influence for good. A great Christian, a brave and lovable man, we who knew him so well will always be grateful for his friendship and for the example that he set.'

Since the photographer had taken nearly 42,000 pictures during his long life, it is hardly surprising to learn that one of these shows the Jesuit burial-plot in Glasnevin Cemetery, Dublin, where Father Browne now rests in peace.

The *Titanic* Photographs in Context

If I had been writing this introduction ten years ago, I would have said that the most newsworthy fact about Father Browne was that he sailed on the *Titanic*. That is no longer the case. The most interesting fact now is that he is being recognised as one of the world's greatest photographers of all time. Let me explain how this came about.

When he died in 1960 Father Browne's trunkful of negatives was deposited in the archives of the Irish Jesuits in Dublin. Twenty-five years passed. In 1985 I had reason to consult the archives and spotted the old trunk which lay buried beneath a multitude of files and documents. On unearthing the trunk, I read the words 'Father Browne's Photographs' chalked on its lid. The inscription meant little to me, because the priest had died shortly after I joined the Jesuits myself. I did remember hearing that a priest called Browne had been on the maiden voyage of the *Titanic* and knew that his album of photographs was kept in a safe. I had no idea that he had taken so many other pictures. You can imagine my amazement, then, when I opened that trunk and found it packed with wallets of negatives, all neatly captioned and dated. The first pack I examined contained photographs of Pompeii (Italy) and La Linea (Spain), dated 1925. These were taken, as I know now, on the return journey from Australia.

The photographs looked superb to me and immediately I thought of having them published. Wolfhound Press in Dublin took a similar view and published its first selection in 1987. A volume has appeared annually ever since. That first book took the critics by storm and quickly it became a best-seller in Ireland. Many experts in photography came to view the Browne Collection. The first of these, David Davison (Head of the Department of Photography in Dublin's Institute of Technology), explained that it would be essential – and costly – to transfer the negatives from their nitrate base to safety-film before the images disintegrated. Thanks to generous sponsorship from Allied Irish Bank this work was soon put in train. The Collection has now been saved and the captions indexed by computer.

Ark Life (Allied Irish Bank's assurance subsidiary) began mounting annual exhibitions of Father Browne's work in 1992; to date the prints have been shown in nearly eighty cities and towns throughout Ireland. In 1993 the Guinness brewery mounted a large exhibition of the Dublin pictures in its Hopstore Gallery. In 1994 RTE (Ireland's national television service) aired six half-hour documentary programmes on the Collection. This series, entitled *The Day Before Yesterday*, was successful and re-broadcast.

Since Christmas of 1995 when Wolfhound Press published *Father Browne's Australia*, the Collection has been earning international recognition. The Australian book rapidly sold out. At Easter 1996, a French book of Browne's photographs came from the press of Anatolia Editions, Paris. This coincided with the opening of a magnificent exhibition of Father Browne's work at the Georges Pompidou Centre in Paris. President Jacques Chirac of France and President Mary Robinson of Ireland were among the 600,000 people who went to see *L'Irlande du père Browne* before it left the French capital for further viewings at Montpellier in the Midi and Lorient in Brittany.

During the Autumn of 1996 Allied Irish Bank gave a display of Browne's prints in Germany, in conjunction with the Frankfurt Book Fair; and towards the end of that year Wolfhound Press published *Father Browne's England*. Another major exhibition which is to open in London and then tour the world is currently being planned.

In the exhibitions to date only half-a-dozen of Father Browne's *Titanic* photographs have been shown to the public. Others have appeared in recent *Titanic* books but the entire set has not been seen till now. Taken by 'a master photographer with an unerring eye' – to quote the London *Independent* art critic – these 1912 pictures, readers will realise, represent some of Father Browne's early work as a photographer. Although he began taking pictures in 1897, his Collection contains only about eight hundred negatives dated before 1912 whereas the bulk of the other 41,000

photographs were taken between 1924 – when the priest went on his rest-cure to Australia and had the leisure to practise his skills in earnest for two full years – and 1954 when old age began to steal up on the old soldier.

When a few of these *Titanic* photographs appeared in newspapers around the world after the liner sank, the focus, naturally, was on the disaster. Eighty-five years later, however, the images take on a new significance when we can view them not only for their inherent documentary interest but as early works from the hand of a man who went on to become a master of the art of photography.

Frank Browne and the Sea
One of the most important facts of Frank Browne's life was that his Uncle Robert was Bishop of Cloyne in the south of Ireland. The bishop's residence stood beneath the Cathedral of St. Colman in Queenstown (now Cobh), the transatlantic port. It was Bishop Browne who added to the cathedral the tallest spire in Ireland which was the last glimpse of their native land to be seen by thousands of departing emigrants.

As a child Frank spent the summer months in his uncle's house and even in later life he took many vacations there. His brother, William, was the bishop's secretary and his sister, Nell, was the bishop's housekeeper. Frank obviously felt at home in Queenstown which was an extremely busy port before the age of air travel. Even today the harbour has a distinguished yacht club and plays host to many cruise liners (such as the *Queen Elizabeth II*) and to the Tall Ships Race. When Frank Browne was a young man it was even busier: besides being a passenger station it was a major base of the Royal Navy. As a so-called 'Treaty Port', it remained in British hands until 1938, sixteen years after Ireland had gained its independence.

Young Browne was a familiar figure on the quayside and, because of his episcopal relationship, had free entrée into areas debarred to the general public. He became friendly with the masters of the two Queenstown tenders, *America* and *Ireland*, who brought him out to the liners and let him photograph them while they were trans-shipping passengers and mail. He also knew the master of the Tug *Flying Sportsman* who taught him the principles involved in releasing the smaller liners from the Queenstown wharves.

As a result of all this, the Browne Collection contains photographs of ships from many different countries.

From the era of sailing ships there are pictures of the *Atacama* (Denmark), *Archibald Russell* (Great Britain), *C.B. Peterson* (Australia) and *Mercator* (Belgium) to mention but four.

From the steam age we have the American Line's *Haverford* and *Philadelphia,* the German ship *Hertzognen Cecilia,* the Inman Line's *City of Paris* and the Anchor Line's *Californian.* Royal Navy vessels include the HMS *Inflexible* and the Admiralty Yacht *Enchantress* with Mr Winston Churchill on board.

When transatlantic liners became bigger and faster in the early decades of this century, the greatest rivalry emerged between the White Star Line and Cunard. Vying for a greater share of the market, the former lured passengers by stressing the luxury of their appointments, the latter by the speed of their ships. Father Browne points out this distinction in his captions.

Of course the passengers who could afford to pay for speed also expected excellent accommodations. The Cunarders as well as the White Star liners were veritable floating palaces, as evidenced in the Browne photographs. The Collection shows the Cunard Line's *Caledonia, Franconia, Laconia, Lusitania* and *Mauretania.* The White Star is represented by the *Arabic, Adriatic, Baltic, Celtic, Megantic* and *Oceanic* as well as by the *Titanic* and her sister ship *Olympic.*

On the Day a Liner Sailed

Before a liner left Queenstown for America a host of preliminaries had to take place: preparing the cargo and passenger manifests, filling in documents for customs clearance, unloading mailbags at the railway station off a train bringing post from throughout the United Kingdom, checking departing passengers through the emigration authorities, and so on. As a final hurdle before boarding the tender, passengers were interviewed by a United States Consul and those intending to remain in that country had to have their eyes examined for trachoma by an American doctor.

Queenstown bustled with life on the day of a sailing. Porters jostled for jobs; White Star officials attended to the special needs of infants and the infirm; vendors and hawkers plied what Frank Browne called 'Legal and Illegal Trade'; American ladies bought their last samples of Irish lace. All of this was accompanied by the sound of the local Pipe Band and when the tenders were leaving the liner, having delivered passengers, cargo and mail, a lone trumpeter played a final salute.

In 1912, when Frank Browne was leaving Waterloo Station in London on the morning of 10th April on board the *Titanic* Special, he would have known that frantic preparations had already been put in motion at Queenstown. Ships were expected from Liverpool and New York that morning, but these now ranked as commonplace occurrences. What exercised everybody's mind was the imminent arrival of the largest liner in the world and the air of excitement was tangible.

I think the best way of concluding this Introduction is to illustrate from Frank Browne's own photographs of various liners the kinds of activity that were taking place in Queenstown before the *Titanic* left Ireland and headed for its doom.

On the Day a Liner Sailed: a Photo Essay

Crowds waiting to embark on the tenders at White Star Wharf, Queenstown.

A view of Queenstown from the tender before the spire was added to St.Colman's Cathedral by the photographer's uncle, Bishop Robert Browne of Cloyne.

Passengers disembarking at White Star Wharf, Queenstown.

Facing: *American ladies disembarking from the tender* America.

Below: *Queenstown vendors had franchises to sell Irish lace and other souvenirs aboard the transatlantic liners.*

Right: *Authorised trader, Mrs Galvin, on the Queenstown wharf awaiting the arrival of passengers.*

Below: *Illegal trade in progress alongside a liner.*

Porters waiting for employment to transfer mails.

Passengers on board a White Star liner watch the mail being transferred.

'A drop in the mail!' Hopefully, no breakables are in the bags being dropped into the hold.

Crewmen loading mail and adjusting a liner's lantern.

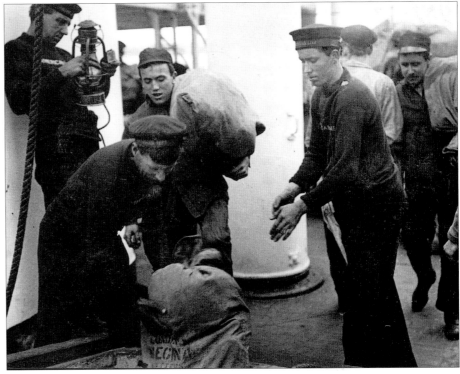

Mail-bags and trunks ready for loading after passengers have boarded.

Loading the mails which had come by rail on the 'American Mail Special' from Cork.

Clockwise, from right:
Second-class passengers embarking from the tender Ireland.
Steerage passengers getting settled on deck.
First-class passengers mount the gangway.
Mother and child receive special attention.

Porter 'spotting form' on the steerage deck. Note the 'English Style' rafts beside the lifeboat at the top of the picture.

U.S. doctor inspecting eyes. No passenger suffering from trachoma or other contagious diseases was permitted to travel.

The tender Ireland *departing from a liner with a small number of passengers.*

The tenders Ireland *and* America *off Deepwater Quay.*

The signal lamps being inspected by a Port of Cork official. Normally this task was carried out by one of the liner's officers.

One of the formalities of the port involved lifeboat drill and the inspection of life-jackets.

White Star Letter, 3 April, 1912

WHITE STAR LINE.

JAMES SCOTT & Co. Agents.

Telegrams: "ISMAY" Queenstown
Telephone Nº 3.

Passenger. Department.

1, COCKSPUR STREET, S.W.
"Oceanic House."
Telegraphic Address: "VESSELS, LONDON."
38, LEADENHALL STREET, E.C.
LONDON.
Telegraphic Address: "ISMAY, LONDON."
CANUTE ROAD, SOUTHAMPTON.
Telegraphic Address: "ISMAY, SOUTHAMPTON."
9, BROADWAY, NEW YORK.
Telegraphic Address: "ISMAY, NEW YORK."
84, STATE ST. BOSTON.
Telegraphic Address: "ISMAY, BOSTON."
118, NOTRE DAME ST WEST, MONTREAL.
Telegraphic Address: "ISMAY, MONTREAL."
21, PIAZZA DELLA BORSA, NAPLES.
Telegraphic Address: "ISMAY, NAPLES."
VIA ALLA NUNZIATA, Nº 18, GENOA.
Telegraphic Address: "ISMAY, GENOA."
PARIS AGENT: NICHOLAS MARTIN, 9, RUE SCRIBE.
Telegraphic Address: "ISMAY, PARIS."
30, JAMES ST., LIVERPOOL.
Telegraphic Address: "ISMAY, LIVERPOOL."

Scott's Square, QUEENSTOWN, April 3rd. 19 12.

"OLYMPIC" TRIPLE SCREW 45,324 TONS
"TITANIC" TRIPLE SCREW 45,000 TONS
THE LARGEST STEAMERS IN THE WORLD

WHITE STAR LINE
SERVICES.

SOUTHAMPTON-CHERBOURG-NEW YORK.
ROYAL & UNITED STATES MAIL STEAMERS.
VIA QUEENSTOWN (WESTBOUND)-PLYMOUTH (EASTBOUND)

LIVERPOOL-NEW YORK.
VIA QUEENSTOWN.

LIVERPOOL-NEW YORK.
(FREIGHT.)

LIVERPOOL-BOSTON.
VIA QUEENSTOWN.

LIVERPOOL-QUEBEC-MONTREAL.

LIVERPOOL-AUSTRALIA.
VIA SOUTH AFRICA.

LIVERPOOL-AUSTRALIA.
(FREIGHT.)

LIVERPOOL-NEW ZEALAND.
(FREIGHT.)

LONDON-NEW ZEALAND.
VIA SOUTH AFRICA.

NEW YORK-MEDITERRANEAN.
VIA AZORES.

BOSTON-MEDITERRANEAN.
VIA AZORES.

THROUGH BOOKINGS
TO ALL PARTS
OF THE WORLD.

Dear Father Browne,   "First Class"
            We have pleasure in handing you
herewith pass from Southampton to Queenstown per
s.s. "Titanic" April 10th, and we trust you will have
an enjoyable trip.

                    Yours truly,
            FOR JAMES SCOTT & Co.,

The Rev. F.M. Browne. S.J.
    Bishop's Palace,
        Queenstown.

Note that despite the letter being addressed to 'Father Browne'
Frank was not a priest at the time. He was due for ordination in 1915.
The Irish mail service was a lot faster in 1912 than it is today. The letter with its precious
enclosure would have been delivered to the Bishop's Palace on the afternoon of the 3rd April
and would certainly have made one of the three Dublin deliveries next day.

CHAPTER ONE

Before Sailing

On 4th April, 1912, Frank Browne received a pleasant surprise in the post: a letter from the White Star Line offices in Queenstown, County Cork, enclosing a first-class ticket for the *Titanic's* maiden voyage from Southampton to Queenstown via Cherbourg. The ticket had been purchased for him by his uncle, Robert Browne, Bishop of Cloyne.

At this point of his formation as a Jesuit, Frank was in the middle of his second year of theological studies at Milltown Park in Dublin. He would have needed special permission from the Rector to absent himself for four days. One suspects that permission would have been refused had a bishop not been involved. It was that same bishop who had armed his nephew with a camera and with a Brief of Pope Leo XIII encouraging the emerging art of photography.

It is interesting to note that the agents of the White Star Line in Queenstown, James Scott & Company, are still in business at the port that is now named Cobh.

On 8th April, Frank travelled to London via Holyhead. It is probable that he spent the night of the 8th on the train south and the night of the 9th with his brother James in London. Dr. James Browne lived just outside of London and was the eldest of Frank's siblings. An eye specialist, he worked at Southwark Hospital in the English capital. He had the dubious honour of signing the death certificate of Bram Stoker, the author of *Dracula*. Bluntly, he gave the cause of death as 'venereal disease'. I am assured that most doctors at that time would have written 'heart failure'.

Early on the morning of 10th April, Frank Browne travelled to Waterloo Railway Station in London to catch what he called the 'first and last *Titanic* Special'.

His own account of the famous journey is given in full in chapter five. Suffice it to say here that he took several photographs before leaving London, one of them captioned 'Mr. Astor to see us off'. That caption – and the controversy surrounding it – will be dealt with in detail in chapter three.

At Southampton railway station the Jesuit was met by his Irish friend, Tom Brownrigg, who accompanied him on board the liner. After taking a photograph on the gangway, Frank Browne was handed a plan of the liner showing the location of the cabins and state-rooms. Measuring a scarcely credible 40 inches by 30 inches, this huge plan was headed 'RMS *Titanic*'.

N.B.
This is really a plan
of the Olympic from which the Titanic
differed in several minor details.

WHITE STAR LINE.
TRIPLE SCREW R.M.S. "TITANIC," 45,000 TONS.
(Combination of Turbine and Reciprocating Engines).
ONE OF THE TWO LARGEST STEAMERS IN THE WORLD.
Length 882.6 Feet—Breadth 92.6 Feet.

PLAN

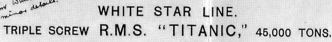

TRIPLE SCREW R.M.S. "TITANIC," 45,000 Tons.

Single Berth Stateroom A 21 and similar, showing type of Bedstead fitted throughout the First Class Accommodation on Boat Deck and Decks A, B, C and D, and Rooms E 1 to E 42, and E 200 to E 203 on Deck E.

NOTES.

RESTAURANT. In addition to the Regular Dining Saloon there is a large modern à la carte Restaurant, on Deck B, where meals may be obtained at any time between 8 a.m. and 11 p.m. at fixed charges, as shown on the bill of fare issued from day to day.

The Restaurant is under the management of the Company, who have appointed Mr. L. Gatti, late of Oddenino's Imperial Restaurant, London, as Manager.

Passengers wishing to use the Restaurant should apply on board to the Manager for the reservation of seats.

If the passage is taken entirely without meals in the regular Dining Saloon, an allowance of £3 per adult will be made of the ocean rate, excepting that on rates of £35 per adult and upwards the allowance will be £5 per adult.

This reduction in fare, however, can only be granted when passengers announce their intention to book without meals, and of making use of the Restaurant, at the time of purchasing their ticket, and no rebate or reduction can be made under any other circumstances.

TURKISH, ELECTRIC AND SWIMMING BATHS. A fully-equipped Turkish Bath is situated on Deck F, consisting of the usual steam, hot, temperate, shampooing, and cooling rooms. Electric Baths and a Swimming Bath are also provided in conjunction with same, and experienced attendants will be in charge.

These Baths will be available for Ladies from 10 a.m. to 1 p.m., and for Gentlemen from 2 to 6 p.m., tickets being obtainable at the Enquiry Office at a charge of 4/- (or 8s.) each.

The Swimming Bath will be open for Gentlemen from 6 to 9 a.m., free of charge.

A GYMNASIUM, fully supplied with modern appliances, is situated on the Boat Deck, and is open for exercise by Ladies and Gentlemen during the same hours as the Baths, no charge being made for the use of the appliances.

The Gymnasium will be available for Children from 1 to 3 p.m. only.

A SQUASH RACQUET COURT is provided on Deck F, and is in charge of a professional player. Tickets for the use of the Court may be obtained at the Enquiry Office at 2/- (or 50 cents) per hour, to include the services of the Professional, who is also authorised to sell and hire racquets.

The Court may be reserved in advance by application to the Professional in charge, and may not be occupied for longer than one hour at a time by the same players if others are waiting.

Balls may be purchased from the Professional.

A CLOTHES PRESSING AND CLEANING ROOM is in charge of an expert attendant, who will carry out any work of this kind for Ladies or Gentlemen, in accordance with a fixed printed tariff of charges which can be had on application to the Bedroom Steward.

LOUNGE AND RECEPTION ROOMS. These rooms are situated on Deck A and at the entrance to the Main Dining Saloon on Deck D respectively. They are intended for the use of both Ladies and Gentlemen, and afternoon tea and after-dinner coffee will be served, while liqueurs, cigars and cigarettes may be purchased there.

Books may be obtained from the Bookcase in the Lounge on Deck A on application to the Steward in charge.

By special arrangement with "The Times" Book Club, a supply of recent works is placed on board each voyage, as a supplement to the permanent collection of standard works.

The Lounge will be closed at 11.30 p.m. and the Reception Room at 11 p.m.

PASSENGER ELEVATORS.—There are three elevators provided for the use of Passengers, running between Decks A, B, C, D and E.

VERANDAH CAFÉ AND PALM COURT situated on Deck A, where light refreshments are served.

ELECTRIC HEATERS (under control of passenger) are fitted in all Staterooms on Boat Deck and Decks A, B, C and D, and in Staterooms E 1 to E 64, and E 200 to E 203 on Deck E.

INDEX.

W.—INDICATES WARDROBE.
W.B.—   WASH BASIN.
D.T.—   DRESSING TABLE.
D.—   CHEST OF DRAWERS.
W.T.—   WRITING TABLE.

ALL STATEROOMS on Boat, A, B, C, D Decks are fitted with HOT AND COLD WATER SUPPLY.
STATEROOM NUMBERS IN RED.
BERTH NUMBERS IN BLACK.
ODD NUMBERS ARE LOWER BERTHS.

December, 1911.

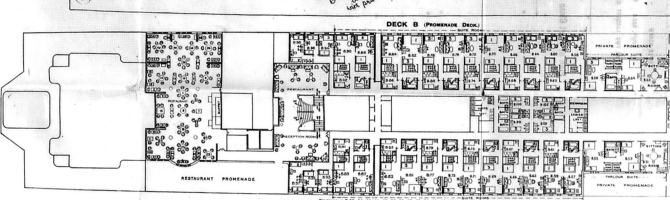

DECK A (UPPER PROMENADE DECK.)

DECK B (PROMENADE DECK.)

Staterooms B 53, 54, 55, 56, 57, 58, 59, 60, 63, 64, 65, 69, 70, 71, 72, 73, 76, 77, 78, 79, 80, 82, 83, 84, 87, 88, 89, 90 are fitted with 4 feet wide Bedstead (No. 1).

DECK C (UPPER DECK.)

Staterooms C 57, 59, 61, 63, 64, 65, 66, 67, 68, 69, 70, 71, 72, 73, 74, 75, 76, 77, 78, 79, 80, 81, 82, 83, 84, 85, 86, 87, 88, 89, 90, 91, 92, 93, 94, 96, 98, 100, 102 are fitted with 4 feet wide Bedstead (No. 1).

The portholes on Deck C are 40 feet above the Water Line.

DECK D (SALOON DECK.)

DECK F (MIDDLE DECK.)

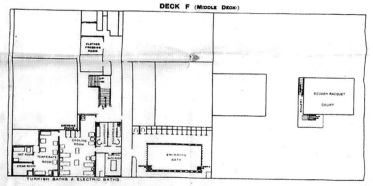

BOAT DECK.

DECK E (MAIN DECK.)

Staterooms with Berths numbered 1, 2 and 3 are fitted with Two Fixed Berths and Sofa Berth (No. 3).
Staterooms E 47, 48, 57, 58, 59, 60, 61, 62, 63 are fitted with one Fixed Lower Berth (No. 1) and a Pullman Upper Berth (No. 2).

The portholes on Deck E are 30 feet above the Water Line.

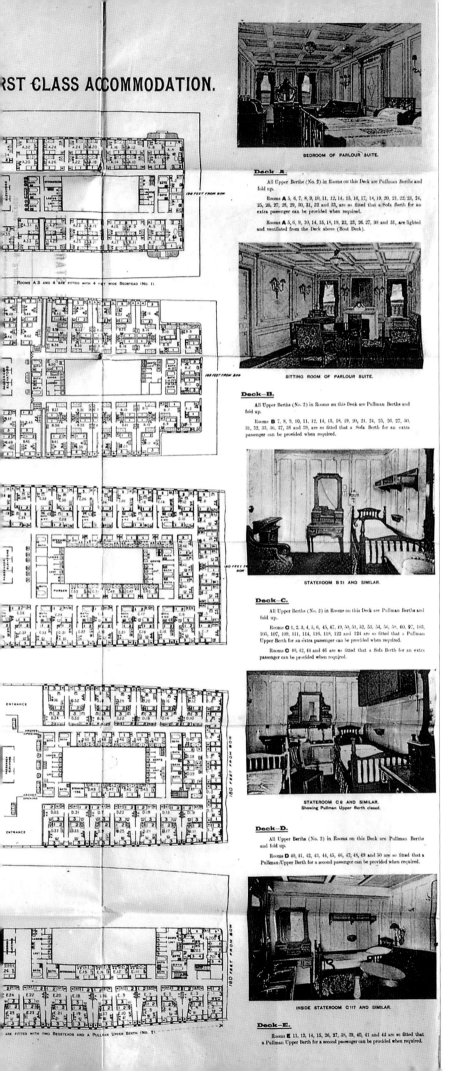

Browne's Copy of the Plan of the Liner

The curious thing about this is that Frank Browne thought that the plan was not of the *Titanic*! As can be seen from his notes and additions, page 32, he believed it was a plan of the sister ship *Olympic*, which differed in several respects. State-rooms 36A and 37A did not exist on the plan, so Frank penned them in. His own state-room was number 37A; number 36A was for Mr. Thomas Andrews, Managing Director of Harland and Wolff, Belfast, the liner's builders. The fact is that this is an early plan of the *Titanic*, dated December 1911. Although it did not show these state-rooms, it did show a restaurant and some B-deck cabins that were not on the *Olympic*.

The reader will notice that in his own account of the voyage (chapter five) Frank Browne made no reference to these interesting lacunae. In January 1997, I had the pleasure of visiting the Marine Museum at Fall River, Massachusetts. On the walls there I saw plans of both the *Titanic* and the *Olympic*. The latter shows two state-rooms where Frank Browne had to add them. Numbered 46A, curiously, and 37A, these must have been added to the *Olympic's* accommodations when the liner was returned to Belfast for modification after the *Titanic* disaster.

When Dr. Robert Ballard and his team found the wreck of the *Titanic*, they were able to verify that those survivors who had affirmed that the liner split in two before sinking were correct. The wreck of the ship lies in two sections that are almost two thousand feet apart. It is uncanny to notice that the *Titanic* split directly through state-rooms numbered 36A and 37A.

A final word on the plan that Frank Browne amended. The reader will be able to see, vaguely, that it carried seven pictures. These will be shown, enlarged, in chapter four of this book. Even though these illustrations are really of the *Olympic*, they show several features that were identical on the *Titanic*. We are including them in this book not just because they were on the plan that Frank Browne was handed when he boarded the liner but also because they will give the reader some additional pictorial information on the interior of the ship and its furnishings.

The handwritten notes on this plan are reproduced overleaf.

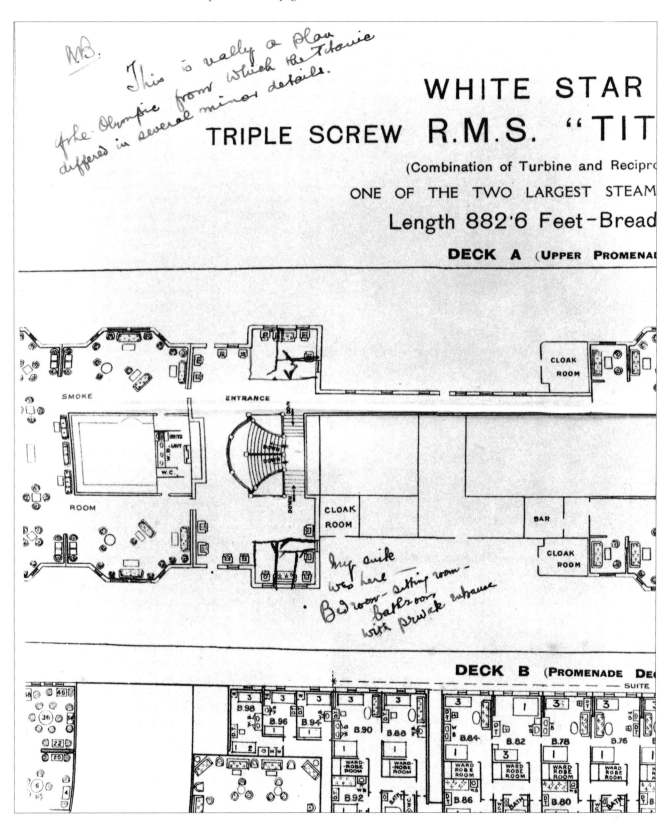

N.B.

This is really a plan of the Olympic from which the Titanic differed in several minor details.

WHITE STAR

TRIPLE SCREW R.M.S. "TIT

(Combination of Turbine and Recipr

ONE OF THE TWO LARGEST STEAM

Length 882·6 Feet—Bread

DECK A (UPPER PROMENA

SMOKE

ENTRANCE

CLOAK ROOM

ROOM

CLOAK ROOM

BAR

CLOAK ROOM

My suite was here — Bedroom — sitting room — bathroom with private entrance

DECK B (PROMENADE DE

SUITE

CHAPTER TWO

The *Titanic* Album Facsimiles

Father Browne put together his *Titanic* album in the year 1920. As already explained in my introduction, the volume contained photographs of many other ships besides the famous liner. Altogether, the album comprises 63 pages with a total of 159 photographs. It also contains press cuttings and other printed memorabilia.

Originally, Father Browne pasted his photographs on separate sheets of cream-coloured mount-board and added his captions in handwriting. Then he gave these sheets to a book-binder who trimmed the pages before binding them together in a heavy leather cover. Unfortunately, some of the captions were cut off during this trimming process. In most cases, however, the missing words can be supplied from the immediate context.

It should be noted that the album, unlike the rest of the Browne Collection, was never 'lost'. While the trunkful of 42,000 negatives lay buried in the Jesuit archives in Dublin, the album was kept in a safe by Fr. John Guiney SJ, treasurer of the Jesuit Order in Ireland. He knew that the album was a valuable asset, although even he was surprised when a London newspaper, after taking professional advice, valued the album at two million pounds sterling. Apart from the album itself, however, the rest of the material that appears in this book *was* in the now famous trunk and temporarily lost.

The pages that follow show most of the leaves of the album that relate to the *Titanic*, including the ones taken at Waterloo Railway Station in London prior to the departure of the train for Southampton. The reader will need to know in advance that chapter three will show these photographs in enlarged format and will comment on Father Browne's captions, correcting some of them and expanding on others.

THE NEW WHITE STAR LINER "TITANIC" (45,000 TONS) NEARING COMPLETION:
DOCKED IN THE LARGEST GRAVING DOCK IN THE WORLD. BELFAST, FEBRUARY 1912.

Photo by
Walton
57 Royal Aven.
Belfast

The first

Unclouded Hours

of

This Card was purchased from the Lounge Steward
on board the Titanic.

The "Titanic's"

Life

WHITE STAR LINER R. M. S. "TITANIC" LAUNCHED 31ST MAY 1911,
SUNK OFF CAPE RACE ON MAIDEN VOYAGE, 15TH APRIL 1912, 1565 PASSENGERS LOST.

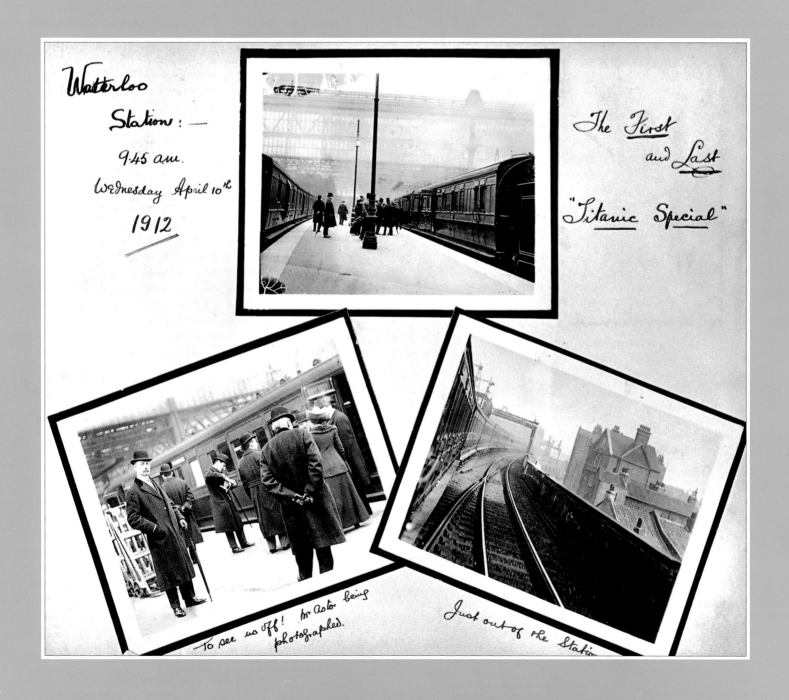

Watterloo
Station :—
9.45 a.m.
Wednesday April 10th
1912

The First
and Last
"Titanic Special"

To see us off! Mr Astor being photographed.

Just out of the Station

As seen from Saloon Gangway.
In the distance can be seen the Second Class
Gangway about 150 feet away.

As seen from the "Boat Deck"
"St Louis" "Philadelphia" (American Line) &
"Majestic" lying in dock beside
Titanic

In Dock

Tugs beginning to strain

Waving good bye. Station & Docks as
seen from Boat Deck of Titanic.

The Start

" Scarce four hundred yards down the jetties were
" moored two other great liners, the "Oceanic" &
" the "New York". The "New York" being on the
" Outside was thronged with sightseers eager to cheer
" the great ship on her maiden trip. we on the
" Titanic" crowded the sides to return their salutes. x

Suddenly there was a crack, followed by a stampede
Of the sightseers on the "New York", then four more cracks
like pistol shots in quick succession, & the great 10,000 ton
liner, her steel cables having al snapped like thread,

drifted from her moorings, drawn into the
fairway, by the wash of the "Titanic".

The "New York"

ceased, but on came the helpless "New York." Tugs blew their syrens, & rushed to her aid, but on she came. A voice beside me said "Now for a crash", & I snapped my shutter. Then we rushed aft along the deck to see what would happen, but only to see the black hull of the "New York" glide gently past, out into the open space where a few seconds before had been the stern of the "Titanic."

Soon the Tugs drew in the broken cables, and the "New York" was towed slowly past us. Even then however she was not out of the way, for when the "Titanic" reversed her engines, to give a little more room, once more the "New York" was drawn across our bows. It was but for a moment, & then we slowly forged ahead down Southampton Water, with the Channel open & free before us." (from Belvederian 1912)

Bells clanged from the Bridge of the "Titanic" & far away aft the churning of the propellers

Incident

THE "TITANIC" LEAVING SOUTHAMPTON DOCKS, 10 APRIL 1912

F. J. Arnott, Photo.

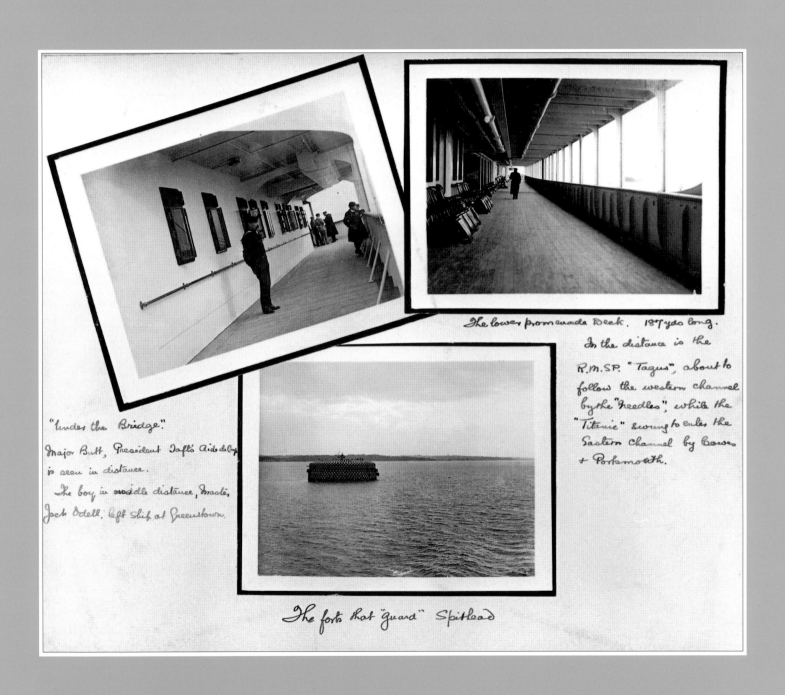

"Under the Bridge".
Major Butt, President Taft's Aide de Camp,
is seen in distance.
The boy in middle distance, Master,
Jack Odell, left Ship at Queenstown.

The lower promenade Deck. 187 yds long.
In the distance is the
R.M.S.P. "Tagus", about to
follow the western channel
by the "Needles", while the
"Titanic" swung to enter the
Eastern Channel by Cowes
+ Portsmouth.

The forts that "guard" Spithead

✕

In the Marconi Room.

Mr Harold Bride, afterwards saved, sitting at the table.

Two exposures on the one plate! This is the only photo ever taken of the Marconi room of the "Titanic".

_____

Mr Jack Phillips (on left), who was lost on the Titanic, taken shortly before his transfer from the "Adriatic".

Dropping Anchor at Queenstown (mcL)
12.15 pm. Ap. 11th

The last
Glimpse of
Capt Smith

Seen from the Tender.

(mcL)

Weighing
the Anchor

1.55 pm.
Ap. 11th

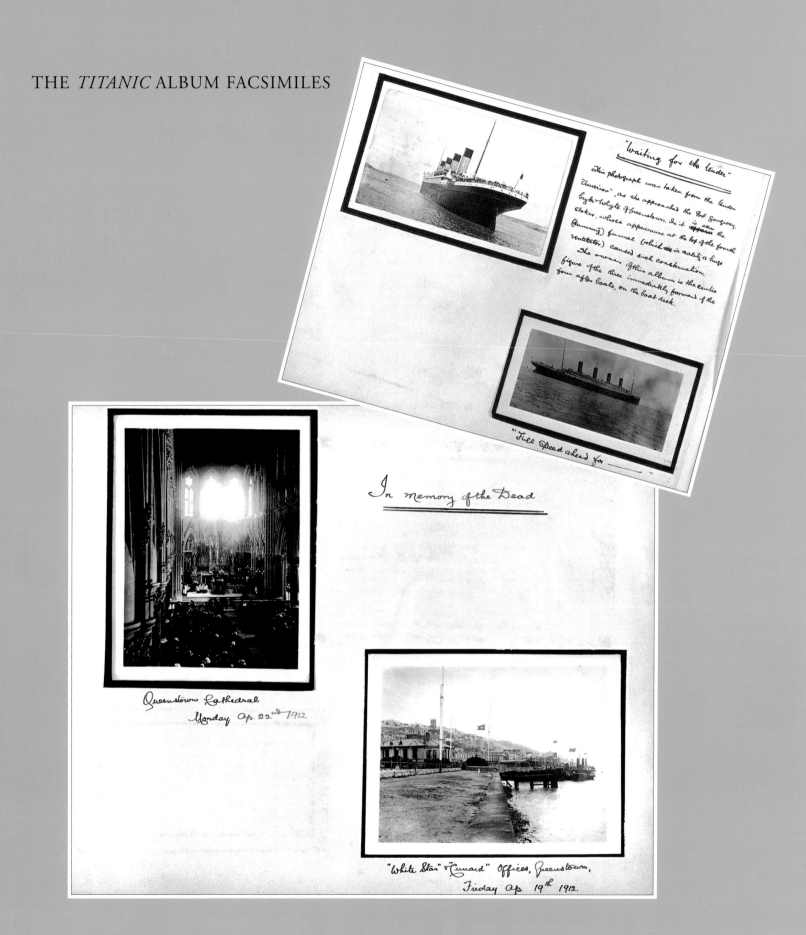

"Waiting for the tender"

This photograph was taken from the tender "America", as she approached the *Port* gangway, by Mr Whyte of Queenstown. In it is seen the stoker, whose appearance at the top of the fourth (dummy) funnel (which is in reality a huge ventilator) caused such consternation. The owner of this album is the centre figure of the three immediately forward of the four after boats, on the boat deck.

"Full Speed ahead for _____"

In memory of the Dead

Queenstown Cathedral
Monday Ap. 22nd 1912

"White Star" & "Cunard" Offices, Queenstown,
Friday Ap 19th 1912.

CHAPTER THREE

This chapter gives enlargements of the photographs in chapter two. Father Browne's captions are annotated and corrected where necessary. For the extra information contained in this chapter I am particularly grateful for the assistance of Mr. Don Lynch and Mr. Ken Marschall of California whose knowledge of the liner and its history are second to none.

Any mistakes that remain, however, should be attributed to me personally.

THE NEW WHITE STAR LINER "TITANIC" (45,000 TONS) NEARING COMPLETION:
DOCKED IN THE LARGEST GRAVING DOCK IN THE WORLD. BELFAST, FEBRUARY 1912.

Although captioned as the Titanic, *this postcard is actually her sister ship* Olympic *under construction at Harland and Wolff Ltd. in Belfast. Normally the most noticeable difference between the two ships was the* Titanic's *enclosed A-deck promenade. However, at this point in their construction, both ships had this promenade open. In this photograph the B-deck promenade is open at the aft end for a greater length than the* Titanic's, *and while on the* Olympic *B-deck was, like A-deck, a promenade, on the* Titanic *it had staterooms with only two short private promenade decks for two of the suites. Quite irresponsibly, it was not unusual for photographs of the* Olympic *to be substituted for the newer, less photographed,* Titanic *when postcards were being produced.*

WHITE STAR LINER R. M. S. "TITANIC" LAUNCHED 31 ST MAY 1911,
SUNK OFF CAPE RACE ON MAIDEN VOYAGE, 15 TH APRIL 1912, 1565 PASSENGERS LOST.

Unlike the previous postcard, this one was purchased after the Titanic disaster, as evident from the printed caption on the face. In this case it is a photograph of the Titanic and not her sister, taken at Harland and Wolff. She appears to be about to set sail on her trials on Tuesday, April 2, 1912. There are tugs waiting at her stern, smoke is coming from her funnels and water is pouring from the condenser exhaust on the side of the ship. Judging by the way the smoke appears as a blur in the photograph, it is apparent that this was a time exposure of at least several seconds.

The caption states that 1,565 passengers were lost in the disaster. This is untrue. Nobody knows exactly how many people lost their lives because there is a great deal of uncertainty as to how many passengers travelled steerage and how many crew members there were altogether. Lists of survivors and of casualties give the same person's name sometimes twice, sometimes three times, with different spellings. All we can say for sure is that a total of over 1,500 people, including crew as well as passengers, lost their lives.

This photograph, and the following two, were taken at Waterloo Station, London. at 9.45 a.m. on Wednesday, 10th April, 1912. The photographer graphically describes the train as 'the first and last Titanic *Special'.*

To capture this image Frank Browne has walked down the platform alongside the Boat Train (right) and has turned to face back towards Waterloo Station to take the photograph. The man in profile on the left appears to be either Stanley or Richard May, two brothers who were travelling with Frank Browne to Queenstown.

For many years it was thought that the gentleman on the left was John Jacob Astor, who perished in the Titanic disaster. Frank Browne's description was apparently accurate, however, when he said, 'To see us off!'; John Jacob Astor was not on the boat train, as he would not board the ship until it reached Cherbourg, France. Recent research has shown that this is his cousin, William Waldorf Astor, who had moved to England from the United States in 1890. Owner of Cliveden and husband of Nancy Astor (the second woman to become a Member of Parliament), W. W. Astor would become Parliamentary Secretary to Lloyd George during World War I and in 1919 would inherit his father's viscountcy.

Frank Browne said the Boat Train left Waterloo Station at 9:45 a.m., yet several other Titanic *passengers recalled afterward that the train departed as early as 8:00 a.m. Presumably, the 'Special' was a non-stop express.*
Here the photographer has leaned far outside the window of the train as it rounds a curve immediately upon leaving the station. This same daring positioning of the camera would be used several times in later photographs.

As he is just about to board the Titanic, Frank Browne has taken this image looking down the length of the ship. In the distance is the second-class gangway, identical to the one on which he is standing. The two structures were built specifically for passengers to board the Olympic, Titanic *and their forthcoming third sister,* Gigantic – *subsequently named* Britannic – *which were all much taller than any ship in existence. The third-class passengers are boarding from a lower gangway, which is slightly below wharf level. On the dock the massive bollards, apparently freshly coated with glossy paint, reflect the sunlight. These bollards, and the railroad tracks, are still on the wharf today although the terminal building is long gone. The large square portholes in the upper left are the private promenade deck of the suite occupied by Mr. J. Bruce Ismay, Managing Director of the White Star Line. Only two of the suites on the ship had their own promenades.*

These three ships, the Saint Louis *and the* Philadelphia *(both of the American Line) and the* Majestic *(White Star Line), had their voyages cancelled by the coal strike which had occurred in England that Spring. Their coal was used for the* Titanic. *Their passengers, and many of their crewmen, were also transferred to the new White Star liner. At the right of the photograph a tug is approaching, so we know that the ship is just casting off. This view is apparently looking aft from the starboard boat deck at the moment of departure.*

Frank Browne has now turned from taking the previous photograph and is facing forward. He has leaned out over the side of the ship with his camera to capture more of the tugs below. In the distance is the far shore of the River Test, with some private yachts at anchor in between. On the left of the photograph is lifeboat number seven. It would be the first to be launched as the ship sank.

The tugs in the foreground, as will be seen more clearly on page 54, are Neptune and Hector.

Moving over to the port side of the boat deck, Frank Browne captures a crowd of mostly local citizens seeing the liner off. This is one of the few known photographs of the new terminal building in its original paint scheme. Completed in 1911, the building would soon after be painted in London and Southwestern Railway's green livery.

The Ocean Terminal still exists at Southampton today but the railway station has been demolished. Different cranes are now at work but the quayside bollards remain unchanged.

The photographer has now moved over to the starboard bow of A-deck where the tugs Hector *and* Neptune *can be seen nudging the ship's bow. In the distance the stern of the liner* New York *has swung out in front of the* Titanic. *On the forward well deck, third-class passengers and off-duty crewmen also watch what is happening below.*

This is the only known clear photograph of the Titanic's Forecastle deck. Because this part of the ship was the first to sink under the sea, and did so slowly, it is largely intact on the bottom of the ocean. All of the fittings visible in the photograph are on the wreck today, including the kedge anchor, which is still bracketed securely to the deck as shown here. Even the railings are the most intact of any on the wreck. The large capstan is where Dr. Robert Ballard deposited a memorial plaque during his dives to the Titanic in 1986.

Once again the camera is held out from the side of the ship. Either Frank Browne himself is leaning far out, or he is holding the camera at arm's length. The Titanic *has already rounded the end of the jetty where, as it passed the American liner* New York, *the latter broke free from its moorings and began to swing toward the larger ship. The photograph was taken from the port side of the boat deck, and below on A-deck, passengers can be seen leaning out from the large promenade deck windows to see the anticipated collision. Like many of the other ships docked in Southampton, the* New York's *voyage had been cancelled by the coal strike.*

The New York *is being pushed by a tug into a temporary position at the end of the quay. Behind it the* Oceanic, *also in dock due to the coal strike, can be seen at its moorage. This is the only Frank Browne photograph in this sequence in which the* Oceanic *appears. Minutes earlier the* New York *was moored alongside it. Both ships, when new, were among the largest liners in the world, and yet it is obvious how they are dwarfed by the* Titanic.

This is the third and last of Frank Browne's valuable postcards. The photograph, taken by F. J. Arnott, shows the tug Vulcan *alongside the* Titanic. *The ship was delayed for an hour on leaving Southampton after its near collision with the* New York. *This delay has always been attributed to the close call itself, yet this photograph shows the bow of the* New York *as it is being swung back into position alongside the* Oceanic. *Clearly the crisis is over. Frank Browne's description of this incident in* The Belvederian – *see chapter five* – *coupled with this photograph, offers a more likely explanation. Some workmen had failed to heed the 'All Ashore' call, and, taking advantage of the ship's stopping after her narrow escape, the* Vulcan *had to be summoned to take them off. The tug is difficult to see in this postcard, but it is lashed to the* Titanic *beneath funnels three and four.*

THE 'TITANIC' LEAVING SOUTHAMPTON DOCKS, 10 APRIL 1912

On A-deck, just below the bridge, Frank Browne snaps the only known photograph of this section of deck on either the Titanic or Olympic. *The boy on the right is Jack Odell, another member of the family with whom Frank Browne is travelling, and in the distance is Major Archibald Butt, military aide to President William Howard Taft. Overhead, a box-like structure conceals the mechanical linkages for the bridge instruments, while on the left are stateroom windows made of particularly heavy-duty brass to withstand any rough weather the ship may face.*

Still on A-deck, Frank Browne has crossed over to the port side and walked aft. This image was taken right at the point where the enclosed section of deck gives way to open promenade. The curve on the railing at right shows where the enclosed windows begin. The cable which stretches above the railing is for a canvas shade, which appears in photographs taken later at Queenstown. The lone figure on the 187-yards-long deck has been described as Captain Smith, yet Frank Browne's album makes no mention of this; a comment he would not have overlooked. It is also highly unlikely that the Captain would not have been on board the bridge with the harbour pilot as they still have not reached open water.

In the distance is the Portuguese ship, RMSP Tagus, which is about to follow the Solent's western channel by the Needles. The Titanic itself will swing left to follow the eastern channel by Cowes and Portsmouth.

Right: One of the forts that guard Spithead – No Man's Land fort in the Solent. This is one of the three sea-forts, known as 'Palmerston's Follies', that guard Portsmouth. The armament was two 6-inch breech-loading guns and two 4.7-inch. The fort was manned by two officers and 27 other ranks. An interior artesian well supplied 1,400 gallons of water per hour. Although they were of considerable strategic importance during both World Wars, none of these forts ever fired a shot in anger.

Looking aft from the port side of the boat deck, the channel fort in the previous photograph has now been left astern. Newspapers described this as dropping the pilot at Portsmouth, where he will be taken ashore by an Isle of Wight boat. This may be based upon Frank Browne's description that this shows the pilot boat coming to take the pilot. Judging by the ship's wake which shows that the Titanic is apparently under way and moving quite quickly, the probability is that the pilot has already been dropped.

Once again Frank Browne is leaning over the railing to take his picture. The lifeboat shown is number ten. This is one of very few photographs of a Titanic lifeboat so clear as to show the ship's name. 'S.S. Titanic' appears on the outboard side, and 'Liverpool' on the inboard.

This is apparently American short story writer Jacques Futrelle, standing on the boat deck outside the Titanic's gymnasium. The author of the popular 'Thinking Machine' mysteries, he had a number of unpublished stories on board with him which would be lost forever. Having turned thirty-seven only the day before sailing, he would lose his life in the disaster.

On the right can be seen lifeboat seven again, the first to be launched after the collision. In the distance, on the roof of the officers' quarters, is collapsible lifeboat A, which would be the last to leave the ship. Floating from the deck, it would be swamped and would rescue only a handful of people, including the only woman to swim away from the ship and survive.

In the centre of the photograph is the illuminated sign-box which identifies the first-class entrance. Just inside is the beautiful grand staircase, with its carved panelling and dome overhead. The windows on the left are those of the ship's gymnasium into which Frank Browne is about to step. Curiously, some of the handrails between the windows have not been installed.

The gentleman in the white flannels is T. W. McCawley, the thirty-four-year-old 'physical educator' from Aberdeen. Another cross-channel passenger would years later recall McCawley as 'rather strict in general with the passengers' but that he softened his demeanour for the children on board. Under his charge is the room filled with the most modern gymnasium equipment available. Unlike many sterile gymnasiums of today, the walls are white-painted pine, with an oak-panelled wainscotting. On the right is an illuminated glass painted map showing the routes of White Star liners around the world.

    The man in the far corner may look like he is enjoying riding the mechanical camel, but he likely considers himself hard at work. He is electrician William Parr, one of the representatives of Harland and Wolff shipbuilders travelling first-class for this maiden voyage. The electrically driven camel had received quite a workout from people touring the ship at Southampton, and William Parr may be ensuring that it continues to work properly. Both men would perish in the sinking, Mr. Parr being survived by his wife of less than two years and a tiny baby. The final two words of Frank Browne's caption (page 40) read: 'Both lost'.

The Titanic's *first sunrise.*
Taken near Land's End, Cornwall,
on the voyage between Cherbourg
and Queenstown, about 6.45 a.m.
on 11th Aptil, 1912.

As a Jesuit 'scholastic' (i.e. student for
the priesthood), Frank Browne
would have been making his
morning Meditation at this hour.
What better place to make it than on
the deck of the Titanic?

Taken from the aft end of A-deck, this photograph is looking forward toward the rear of the ship's superstructure. On the deck above, a group of second-class passengers stare back at the camera. The Olympic and Titanic were unusual in that second-class passengers, who claimed the very aft end of the boat deck for their promenade space, could look down on first-class people, who had the entire A-deck to themselves. The next deck below is again second-class.

The sliding double doors lead into the starboard Verandah and Palm Court, which would become an unofficial playroom for the small children in first-class accommodation. To the right a small cargo crane is visible and the photographer's reflection can be seen in the window directly in front of the camera.

Stepping forward a few feet, and turning to the left, Frank Browne has encountered an unidentified couple taking an early stroll. The port cargo crane is much more visible here than the starboard one was in the previous photograph. Overhead, deck-chairs are stacked against the railing of the second-class promenade. The absence of clearly defined shadows shows that it was overcast this morning. An unusual facet of this photograph is that it is a double exposure. Barely visible is the wicker furniture of the starboard private promenade, part of a suite occupied by Mrs. Charlotte Drake Martinez Cardeza, a Philadelphia millionairess and big game hunter who had boarded at Cherbourg the previous evening. Flowers, possibly a bouquet wishing her bon voyage, *grace one of the tables. The door leading from this promenade into the first-class entrance-way must have been open for Frank Browne to have taken this image as he surely did not know Mrs. Cardeza.*

This photograph is taken from virtually the same location as the previous one. It is now later in the day and Frank Browne is facing starboard instead of port. In the centre is six-year-old Robert Douglas Spedden of Tuxedo Park, New York, spinning a top while his father, Frederic, watches.

Both father and son, together with Mrs. Spedden and their two servants, would survive the sinking but Frederic's photographs – taken with the camera seen here on shoulder-strap – did not. Three years later Douglas would be struck and killed by a motor-car in Maine, USA, ironically a victim of modern transportation after all. In a similar irony, his father Frederic would later drown, suffering a heart attack in a swimming-pool in Florida in 1947.

Still aft on A-deck, Father Browne has now walked over to the starboard railing and is facing forward. He may be leaning out over the rail, as he has done in order to take other photographs, but given the uneven horizon he is more likely holding the camera out at arm's length. Just above, the bottoms of two lifeboats can be seen. The aft boats were cranked slightly outward to allow more promenade space for second-class passengers on the boat deck above. In the distance, an emergency boat – number one – can be seen hanging over the ship's side. It, and boat two on the port side, were swung completely out immediately after leaving Southampton so that they could be lowered easily in the event someone were to fall overboard. This particular boat would later carry Sir Cosmo and Lady Duff-Gordon to safety the night of the sinking.

Facing: *Taken aboard the* Adriatic *prior to Frank Browne's voyage on the* Titanic, *the photograph shows two wireless operators. The gentleman on the left is Jack Phillips, who would stick to his post on board the* Titanic *summoning rescuers for those who, unlike himself, were leaving the ship in lifeboats. One of the undisputed heroes of the disaster, there are memorials on both sides of the Atlantic erected in his memory. It is ironic that Frank Browne placed this photograph in his album amongst those he took on board the* Titanic *on April 11th, for that was the date of Phillips' twenty-fifth birthday.*

Below: *The wake trailing off to starboard confirms Frank Browne's description of the 'winding pathway o'er the waters', and that an irregular course was being taken in order to test the compasses. He is still on the aft end of A-deck, but has now walked to the railing at the far end where he looks over the well-deck. Some third-class passengers can be seen at the bottom centre of the photograph, while the head of a large cargo crane dominates the lower foreground. The photograph confirms that there was no question of the* Titanic *trying to break any speed record.*

The Titanic's *junior wireless operator, Harold Bride, is shown here at his post. This is another double exposure and one that the photographer was going to throw away until, after the disaster, he learned that it was the only picture ever taken in the liner's Marconi room. The wireless equipment on the* Titanic *was the most modern afloat, and the most powerful of any merchant vessel. She had a guaranteed range of 350 miles, but in actuality could transmit and receive messages at a range of 500 miles during the day and a thousand miles away at night. While at Belfast she had been exchanging messages with stations on the Canary Islands off the coast of Africa, and Port Said in the south-eastern Mediterranean.*

Passengers did not normally enter the wireless room as Frank Browne has done, but deposited their messages and payment for such with the purser's office. They were then sent to the operators by pneumatic tube. This tube can be seen on the right, below which is the basket into which the container holding the messages would drop. Like Jack Phillips, Harold Bride would heroically stay at his post the night of the disaster. Unlike his co-worker, Mr. Bride would have a remarkable escape in that he swam away from the sinking liner as it took its final plunge, and then clung to an overturned collapsible boat with a group of other men until he was rescued the following morning.

Frank Browne described this view as the ship dropping anchor, but the wake at her stern shows her to be still under way. She is surely about to stop, however, for already a gangway door in her hull has been opened, below the forward well deck. The liner's flags fly proudly from masts and stern, while along the A-deck aft promenade can be seen the canvas shade described earlier. This beautiful broadside shot was taken from the tender America *by Mr. McLean.*

Dropping Anchor at Queenstown

Facing: *The tender* America *has now pulled alongside the open gangway door, and looking up, Mr. McLean has photographed Captain Smith looking down from the starboard bridge wing, with the leadsman's platform underneath and slightly forward of him. At the edge of the photograph numerous third-class passengers are looking down at the tender, while first-class passengers watch from the deck below the bridge. The 'emergency' lifeboat number two dominates the photograph.*

Below: *Third-class passengers throng the stern of the ship, where can be seen a sign warning of the danger of the propellers below. A tiny dot at the top of the fourth funnel – which is, in fact, a huge ventilator – is the grimy face of a stoker who climbed up for a bird's eye view of the Irish port, and who to some seemed like the black spectre of death looking down. The superstitious among the passengers saw this as an ill omen. Off to the right is Roche's Point, while on the port side of the ship can be seen 'emergency' lifeboat number two, swung out in case it is needed. This would be the first lifeboat rescued by the* Carpathia.*
This photograph was taken from the tender* America *as she approached the port gangway by Mr. Whyte of Queenstown.
Frank Browne is the centre figure of the three immediately forward of the four aft lifeboats left of centre.*

Facing: *The giant starboard anchor of the* Titanic *is raised for the last time. In Queenstown terms (i.e. using imperial, not U.S. measurements), the liner used a length of six cables of wrought-iron chainwork. A cable measured fifteen fathoms, so it took several minutes for the anchor to come to the surface. Taken at 1.55 p.m. on the 11th April, 1912, the photograph shows the very plates that were prised apart by the iceberg.*

The anchor is now up and the Titanic *is slowly steaming out of the harbour. The sun shade, visible along A-deck in the centre of the ship, will likely be raised before the ship reaches full speed and the resulting wind tears at it.*

This is one of the last photographs ever taken of the ship. The very last one is shown on page 92.

CHAPTER FOUR

Supplementary Pictures

The pictures in this chapter fall into four different categories. First, there are some pictures of the *Titanic* taken by Frank Browne but not included in his album. Presumably he thought their quality to be inferior: they are included here because of their historic interest and for the sake of completion.

Secondly, there are pictures taken by Frank Browne aboard the *Olympic*. We are including them here for two reasons: they show parts of the liner that were identical on the *Titanic* and they show features of the liner, such as the bridge and the swimming-pool, that were not seen in the previous chapter.

Thirdly, we have seven pictures of the interior of the liner,

taken from the plan of the ship that Frank Browne was handed when he stepped on board at Southampton. Although these seven photographs may have appeared elsewhere, they are included here because the reader may not have come across them before. Once again, they show parts of 'the floating palace' that were not seen in chapters two or three.

Finally there is an enlarged detail of one of Frank Browne's photographs made by David Davison of Dublin. This is the last extant picture of Caption Edward Smith and, in order to be faithful to the integrity of the photographer, it is a 'natural' enlargement in the sense that no artificial photo-enhancement technique has been employed.

The Titanic *and the tender* America.

Facing: *The bedroom section of Frank Browne's suite of rooms, numbered A37, aboard the* Titanic. *On page 32 we have seen how he drew in his 'suite': bedroom, sitting-room, bathroom – with private entrance.*

Another view of Frank's bedroom but this time the negative was consigned to his 'morgue' and would probably have been consigned to the trash-can had the liner survived. The photographer thought it too fuzzy to include in his album.

TRIPLE SCREW R.M.S. "TITANIC," 45,000 Tons.

BEDROOM OF PARLOUR SUITE.

Deck A

All Upper Berths (No. 2) in Rooms on this Deck are Pullman Berths and fold up.

Rooms **A** 5, 6, 7, 8, 9, 10, 11, 12, 14, 15, 16, 17, 18, 19, 20, 21, 22, 23, 24, 25, 26, 27, 28, 29, 30, 31, 32 and 33, are so fitted that a Sofa Berth for an extra passenger can be provided when required.

Rooms **A** 5, 6, 9, 10, 14, 15, 18, 19, 22, 23, 26, 27, 30 and 31, are lighted and ventilated from the Deck above (Boat Deck).

Single Berth Stateroom A 21 and similar, showing type of Bedstead fitted throughout the First Class Accommodation on Boat Deck and Decks A, B, C and D, and Rooms E 1 to E 42, and E 200 to E 203 on Deck E.

SITTING ROOM OF PARLOUR SUITE.

Enlargement of the photographs shown on the plan of the liner which Frank Browne was handed as he boarded Titanic.
(See pages 30-31 earlier)

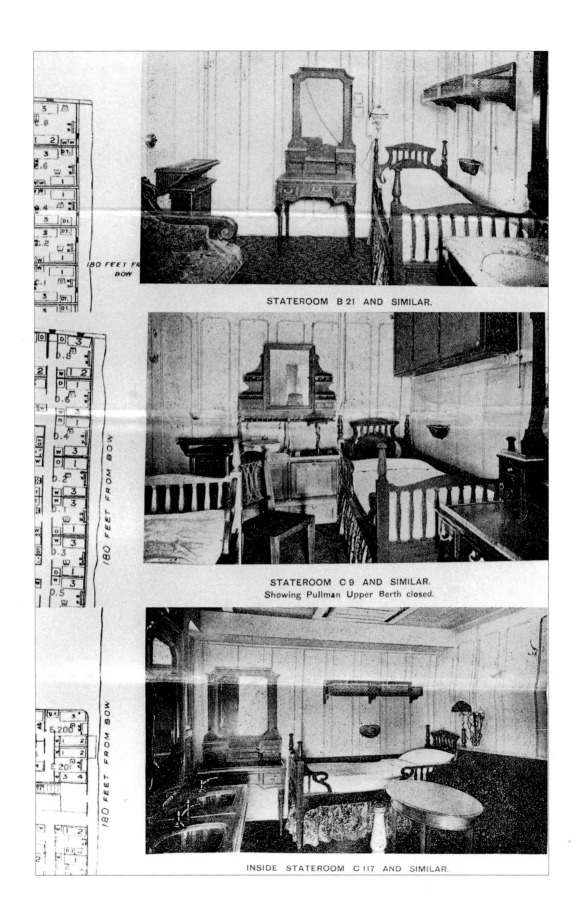

STATEROOM B 21 AND SIMILAR.

STATEROOM C 9 AND SIMILAR.
Showing Pullman Upper Berth closed.

INSIDE STATEROOM C 117 AND SIMILAR.

180 FEET FROM BOW

180 FEET FROM BOW

180 FEET FROM BOW

Right: *The luncheon menu-card for April 14, 1912, which Frank Browne acquired to illustrate his lecture (see page 109).*

The first-class dining room of the Titanic. *Once again, Frank Browne thought it sub-standard and did not include it in his album. It remains, however, one of the few photographs taken in this room. Twenty years later – see page 112 – London's* Daily Express *would do an enhancement job on this picture, removing the central blotch and adding a figure to the right-hand table.*

R.M.S. "TITANIC"

APRIL 14, 1912.

LUNCHEON.

CONSOMMÉ FERMIER   COCKIE LEEKIE

FILLETS OF BRILL

EGG À L'ARGENTEUIL

CHICKEN À LA MARYLAND

CORNED BEEF, VEGETABLES, DUMPLINGS

FROM THE GRILL.

GRILLED MUTTON CHOPS

MASHED, FRIED & BAKED JACKET POTATOES

CUSTARD PUDDING

APPLE MERINGUE   PASTRY

BUFFET.

SALMON MAYONNAISE   POTTED SHRIMPS

NORWEGIAN ANCHOVIES   SOUSED HERRINGS

PLAIN & SMOKED SARDINES

ROAST BEEF

ROUND OF SPICED BEEF

VEAL & HAM PIE

VIRGINIA & CUMBERLAND HAM

BOLOGNA SAUSAGE   BRAWN

GALANTINE OF CHICKEN

CORNED OX TONGUE

LETTUCE   BEETROOT   TOMATOES

CHEESE.

CHESHIRE, STILTON, GORGONZOLA, EDAM,

CAMEMBERT, ROQUEFORT, ST. IVEL,

CHEDDAR

Iced draught Munich Lager Beer 3d. & 6d. a Tankard.

The Reading and Writing Room on A-deck of Titanic. *Frank Browne did not consider the photograph good enough to include in his album, but it is interesting to compare it with the one on page 84.*

Facing: *The Reading and Writing Room on A-deck of* Olympic. *The windows of this room were eleven feet high. The bright band at the top of the windows is the portion of the room which rises above the level of the boat-deck, forming the still higher sun-deck that stood eighty-two feet above the water-line.*

Below: *An excellent interior shot of the* Olympic's *Marconi-room, showing Mr. Brent at work. Compare with the double-exposure shown on page 70. The telephone by which the operator could transmit messages to the bridge, about icebergs ahead or anything else, can be seen just to the right of the Marconi-man's head.*

The bridge of RMS Olympic. *It is worth noting that this is the only known photograph taken of the entire bridge of either* Olympic *or* Titanic. *Other photographs only show small portions of the* Olympic's *bridge – which was practically identical to that of her sister ship. Recent film-sets have been based on this photograph for authenticity.*

Swimming-bath of RMS Olympic, *identical in every respect with that of the* Titanic. *See chapter five for Frank Browne's description of its dimensions. The gentleman at the rear looks like, and may be, the photographer's brother, William, who came to meet the liner. Situated away down on F-deck, this bath adjoined the Turkish Baths and Electric Baths with their state-of-the-art steam-rooms, hot-rooms, temperate-rooms, cooling-rooms and shampooing-rooms.*

Facing: *The Grand Staircase of the* Olympic. *There were seven flights of stairs similar to this, the topmost one. All the woodwork and carving is in pale oak. The carving on the back wall represents 'Honour and Glory crowning Time'.*

Below: *Although frequently stated to be the* Titanic, *this is in fact Frank Browne's last picture of RMS* Olympic *taken from Crosshaven, County Cork. It is included here as an effort to nail a myth.*

David Davison of Dublin made this enlargement of a section of the last photograph of Captain Edward Smith. Due to retire after the Titanic's *return journey from New York*, the captain is seen here gazing, ironically, into the emergency lifeboat.

CHAPTER FIVE

At Sea on the *Titanic*

In 1906, when he went to teach at Belvedere College in Dublin, Frank Browne founded a school journal that is still published annually. For the 1912 issue of *The Belvederian,* he contributed the article on page 93 which was never published elsewhere.

Frank Browne used many of his own photographs to illustrate the article but the first one included was one taken by Thomas Barker of *The Cork Examiner*. Since he was writing for a school readership, the author makes several in-house allusions. I have explained these, as well as some other points that might need explication, by way of endnotes given on page 95.

There are two interesting omissions in the article. The first of these is that Frank Browne makes no mention of the plan of ship that he was handed on boarding. In chapter one we saw that this plan caused great confusion because, although entitled *Titanic*, Browne thought it was in fact a plan of the *Olympic.*

Since he was writing for mainly schoolboy readers, Browne at this time must have made a conscious decision not to tell the story of what he later described as 'the only time holy obedience saved a man's life!'

The story goes that during his voyage on the *Titanic,* Frank was befriended by an American millionaire couple who were seated at the same table in the liner's first-class dining-room. After one of the meals they invited him down to the Marconi-room. They had him send a message to his Superior in Dublin, called the 'Provincial' of the Jesuits, asking permission to remain on board for the remainder of the voyage to New York. The American couple would pay his way.

The message was duly sent and a cabled reply was awaiting Frank Browne when he arrived in Cork Harbour. It consisted of five words:

GET OFF THAT SHIP – PROVINCIAL.

In consequence, when the news of the sinking reached Ireland, Frank Browne was already back at his theological studies in Dublin.

Frank Browne's article in The Belvederian *was illustrated with twelve of his own photographs and one picture courtesy of* The Cork Examiner. *The photograph below is the very last one which Frank Browne took of the departing* Titanic *shortly after 1.55 p.m. on 11 April, 1912.*

At Sea on the *Titanic*

by F. M. Browne S.J.

From *The Belvederian*, 1912

The Southampton Town Clocks had just struck a quarter past twelve on April 9th[1] when the *Titanic* moved away from the Quay. So slowly and gently did she move that as I leaned over the water, I could hardly realise that we were actually in motion. With a feeling akin to suppressed excitement I watched the scene, for it was my first experience of actual travel on an ocean liner, and for a beginning I could not have 'struck' a bigger boat. To convey any idea of her size is difficult. Time and again these ships have been described by professional penmen, each one endeavouring to surpass his predecessors in the wealth and number of adjectives employed.

My first glimpses of the ship had been from the train as it slowly steamed through the streets and the docks of Southampton. At the station I was met by Tom Brownrigg, also an Old Belvederian.[2] Together we started; but it was not till, having ascended three flights of stairs, we stood on the little gangway that gave admission to the Saloon entrance lobby, that we could form any adequate idea of the size of the 'largest ship in the world'.

Left and right stretched a wall of steel that towered high above the roof of the station that we had just left. We were about forty feet above the quay level, and yet scarce more than half way up the side of the ship. Below us the people looked tiny, while some hundred and twenty yards aft we could see the Second-Class passengers crossing the gangway into their portion of the ship.

Once on board a visit to the Purser's office, where a letter of introduction served as a passport to the genial friendship of Mr. McElroy, sent us looking for Cabin A 37, which being translated meant Cabin 37 on Deck A. For those who have no acquaintance with the internal economy of modern liners it may be interesting to note that in the Saloon and Second Class portions of the ship the various Decks or Stories are named A, B, C, and so on, beginning from the top downwards. On the *Titanic* the decks numbered in this way for the Saloon went from A (the promenade deck above which there were

still the Boat and Sun Decks) to E Deck some five stories below. A general description of the arrangements may not be out of place, and will make after events more clear. On the Boat Deck (about 78 feet above the water or a little more than the height of Belvedere House)[3] were situated the Gymnasium and officers' quarters and Bridge. On A Deck were the principal public rooms: the Lounge, which was the finest room ever planned in a ship, with huge bay windows eleven feet high looking out on the promenade deck, the Writing and Reading Room, and the great Smoking Room, the walls of which were made of polished mahogany inlaid with Mother of Pearl. In addition to these public rooms there were about forty staterooms, which, having large windows looking out on the promenade deck were considered among the best on the ship. On B Deck were all the great Suites of rooms which only millionaires could afford to engage. Here were apartments furnished in any style to suit the most exacting taste. Over the doors their names informed you what the style represented: 'Louis XVI', 'Modern', 'Dutch', etc. On C Deck was the great Dining Saloon with the magnificent Reception Room in which there was seating accommodation for nearly six hundred people without any crowding.

D Deck was devoted entirely to staterooms, while on E Deck were situated the Turkish Bath, Racquet Court, Swimming Bath (about half the size of Tara Street Baths)[4], and more staterooms. All these Decks were connected by broad handsome flights of stairs, and by a regular service of Lifts.

Having glanced over this short description, the reader will understand the true significance of the title chosen for this account. Though still beside the Quay, Tom Brownrigg and I were really 'at sea' as we searched for Cabin A 37, and even a steward to whom we applied for guidance could only say, 'That's somewhere aft, Sir'. Eventually we found the cabin, which proved to be a large and very prettily furnished bedroom, with a small private entrance hall and large bathroom attached. Having left there my impedimenta we started to explore the ship as far as time would allow, before the Bugle sounded 'Visitors ashore'. Of course there was no reason for me to hurry, but for Tom the time came all too soon. As the best view was to be obtained from the Boat Deck, I took myself thither as soon as I had said good-bye to Tom. Looking over the side I saw moored close below us three Liners, each of which in its day had been the greatest ship in the world. Nearest to us was the *St. Louis,* next to her the *Philadelphia* (once the *City of Paris*), and beyond her the *Majestic.* How small they looked, and how out of date beside the *Titanic*!

A straining of the tugs attached to the bow and stern of the *Titanic* warned me that we were moving, and crossing to the other side I saw the Quay with its thousands of cheering people gradually dropping astern. Not one of that gay number dreamt that it was their last look at the *Titanic,* and at the friends she bore.

Scarce four hundred yards down the jetties were moored two other great Liners, the *Oceanic,* and the *New York.* The *New York,* being on the outside, was thronged with sightseers eager to cheer the great ship on her maiden trip. We on the *Titanic* crowded the sides to return their salutes. Suddenly there was a crack, a stampede of the sightseers on the *New York,* four more cracks like pistol shots in quick succession, and the great 10,000-ton liner, her steel cables having snapped like thread, drifted from her moorings drawn out into the Fairway by the wash of the *Titanic.* Bells clanged from the Bridge of the *Titanic,* and far away aft the churning of the propellers ceased, but on came the helpless *New York.* Tugs blew their Sirens and rushed to her aid, but on she came. A voice beside me said, 'Now for a crash', and I snapped my shutter. Then we rushed aft along the deck to see what would happen, only to see the black hull of the *New York* glide gently past, out into the open space where a few seconds before had been the stern of the *Titanic.* Soon the tugs drew in the broken cables, and the *New York* was towed slowly past us. Even then, however, she was not out of the way, for when the *Titanic* reversed her engines, to give a little more room, once more the *New York* was drawn across our bows. It was but for a moment, and then we slowly forged ahead down Southampton Water with the Channel open and free before us. A tug came to take ashore the workmen and navvies who had been arranging the luggage in the storerooms, and we were fully off.

Luncheon followed soon, but it was a brief meal, everyone being anxious to be on deck while we steamed down the channel between England and the Isle of Wight.

Here another indication of the size of our ship was given us. Following us down the narrow waterway came the RMPS *Tagus,*[5] on her way to the West Indies. She was a boat of the smaller class, and reaching the point opposite Cowes where the Eastern Channel separates from the Western, she took the course towards the setting sun, a thing that would have been impossible for us, for that channel, though the most direct for ships going southward to the French Coast, as we were, would have been too shallow for the *Titanic,* and consequently we steamed East towards Portsmouth and Ryde, passing on the way many indications of the dreadnought[6] policy, in the shape of lines of 'scrapped' warships lying useless in the roads at Spithead.

'Could you tell me, Sir, why is the Channel so narrow here?' The voice, a loud penetrating one that had not learned its intonation on this side of 'the Herring Pond', came from above me, and I looked up to see whence it proceeded. Its owner was well dressed, and from his appearance of some importance. 'Could you tell me, Sir, why is the channel so narrow here?' he repeated, and I thinking that he referred to the narrow distance between the two chess-board forts that guarded the entrance to Spithead answered, 'I suppose when they built these forts they never calculated on having ships as big as the *Titanic*'.

'Oh, I did not mean that. Why is the land so near here?'

'Well, I suppose, Sir, that they could not shift the Isle of Wight back any further than it is.'

'How far would you say it is from shore to shore here, Sir?'

I looked across and hazarded the answer, 'I should say about ten or twelve miles.'

'Well, how far is it from Dover to Calais?'

'Twenty-one.'

'Why then don't you English cross here?'

A great light dawned on me, and a ghost of a geography lesson in Syntax II[7] classroom seemed to smile upon me from out the past as I replied:

'Oh that's not France, that's the Isle of Wight.'

'I see. I thought it was France', and he moved off. I afterwards photographed him as he stood outside the Gymnasium. [He was Jacques Futrelle, the author.]

And so the afternoon wore on as we steamed down the busy Channel watching the big four-masted sailing ships, and the Cross Channel packets tossing in the choppy sea, while on the *Titanic* there was no indication that the ship was at sea save the brisk cool breeze blowing along the decks, and the swiftly moving panorama of distant coast line.

Owing to the delay caused in starting by the *New York* incident, we did not arrive at Cherbourg till evening was well advanced and while we were saying good-bye to those to whom the excitement of the morning had served as an introduction, and who were getting off at Cherbourg, the bugle sounded the Dinner Call. That I was not the only person 'at sea' on the *Titanic* was proved by the requests made me by some who could not find their way to the Dining Room!

As we sat down to dinner – we were eight at our table – we could see the newly arrived passengers passing in the lobby outside and occasionally hear the busy hum of work as the luggage and mails were brought on board. But soon it all quietened down and after a time someone remarked, 'I wonder have we started yet.' We all stopped for a moment and listened, but noticing no vibration or noise the answer came, 'No, we can't have started yet.' But the waiting steward leant over and said, 'We have been outside the breakwater for more than ten minutes, Sir.' So gentle was the motion of the ship that none could notice its movement (and there was no drink on the table stronger than Apollinaris!!).[8]

After dinner we listened to that orchestra, which in a few days was to win a place in history more tragically glorious than that held by many others of the tragedy of April 15th. But none of us thought of these things then. Those of the passengers who were early astir next morning, and they were many, for the first night at sea is generally a restless one, even when soothed by all the comfort and luxury of a *Titanic*, witnessed the curious evolutions of the Liner as she turned and twisted on a serpentine path while steaming north from the Lizard to Queenstown. It was merely to test the compasses that she did so, and it is a common practice on the ocean-going ships when far from land and not pressed for time.

Then as the day grew older out from the northern horizon the blue haze took a more substantial form and I knew that my brief voyage was drawing to its close.

As we passed Daunt's Rock and slowed up to take the pilot on board from his little tiny boat, someone asked 'What fort is that?'

'Templebreedy, one of the strongest in the kingdom.'

'And do Redmond and his Gang want to take that place?'

'Why do you call them a "Gang," Sir?' was the answer from another. At that moment the Halls at Westminster were filing for the first reading of the Home Rule Bill![9]

Then came the tender and the mails and soon the hour of leaving came for me. As I passed down the gangway I met Mr. McElroy and Mr. Nicholson, Head of the Mail Department on the *Titanic*.

'Goodbye,' I said, 'I will give you copies of my photos when you come again. Pleasant voyage.'

And so they went. They never came back, one dying at his post far down in the heart of the ship as he strove to save the more precious portion of his charge, the other calmly facing death as he strove to reassure the terror-stricken, and to render up the jewels given to his keeping.

Four days passed and then came the awful news, whispered at first, then contradicted, but finally shouted aloud in all its horror of detail by the myriad-throated press.

And here in Ireland, in Queenstown, we did not forget those whom we had seen departing in all the joy of hope and confidence, for we gathered in the great Cathedral to pray for those who had departed, and for those on whom the hand of sorrow had fallen so heavily.

NOTES

1. Actually, it was 10th April 1912.
2. Belvedere College is a Jesuit school in Dublin, *alma mater* of Frank Browne SJ and James Joyce.
3. The Community House at Belvedere College. This five-storey building, completed for Lord Belvedere in 1785, is over seventy-five feet high.
4. Dublin swimming pool measuring twenty-two yards long and twelve yards wide.
5. A Portuguese Mail Ship.
6. The first HMS *Dreadnought* was named and launched by Queen Elizabeth I in 1573. The ninth Royal Navy ship of that name was launched in 1906 and gave its name to subsequent battleships of every nation. By the time Churchill came to the Admiralty in 1911, eighteen British dreadnoughts had been launched. In the 1912 Naval Estimates he sought money for a further five.
7. Syntax II is the name of a college year at Belvedere. It corresponds to third-year in High School.
8. Apollinaris water is a mineral water from the eponymous spring in the Ahr valley of Germany.
9. The Home Rule Bill for Ireland was the issue which dominated the Westminster parliament and the European newspapers in April 1912.

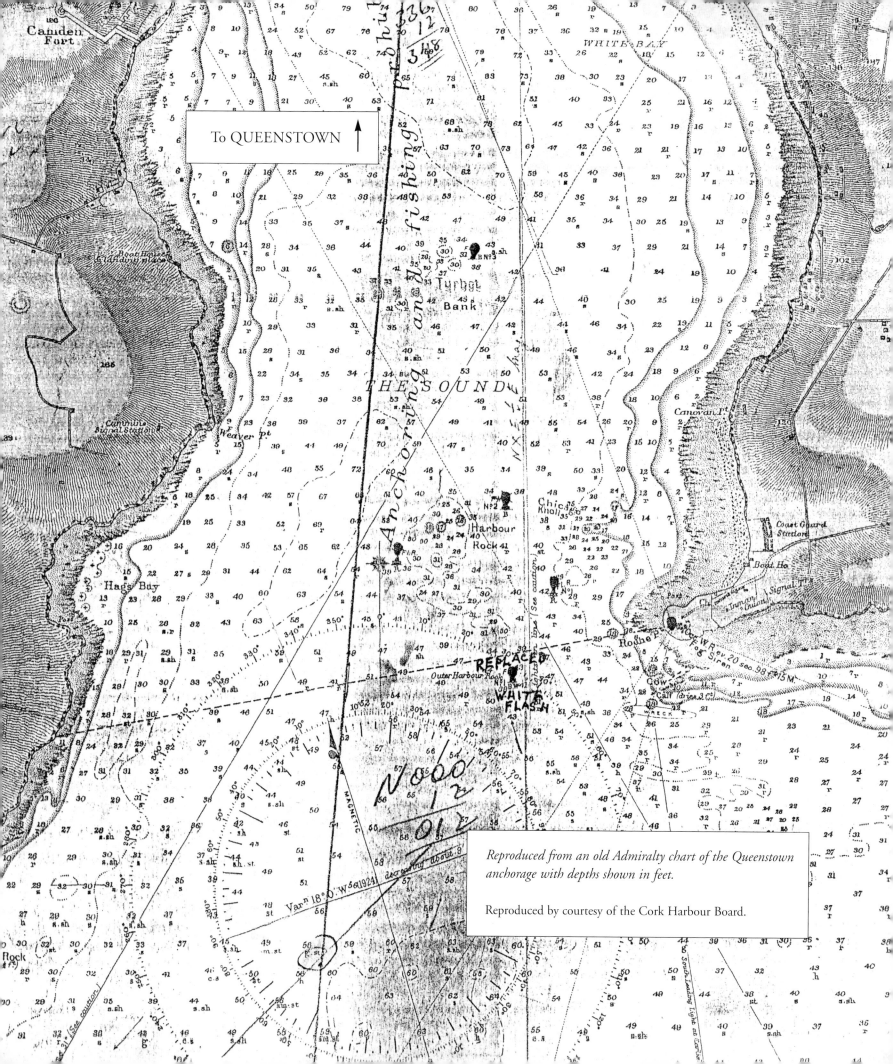

To QUEENSTOWN ↑

THE SOUND

Reproduced from an old Admiralty chart of the Queenstown anchorage with depths shown in feet.

Reproduced by courtesy of the Cork Harbour Board.

CHAPTER SIX

The *Titanic* at Queenstown

At 11.55 a.m. on Friday, 11th April, the *Titanic* reached Cork Harbour in the south of Ireland. The following day's local newspaper, *The Cork Examiner,* described her arrival as follows:

> As one saw her steaming slowly, a majestic monster floating it seemed irresistibly, into the harbour, a strange sense of might and power pervaded the scene. She embodies the latest triumphs in mercantile engineering and although a sister ship of the *Olympic* is an improvement in many respects on the latter.

> Whatever conditions the modern voyager looks for in the vessel which he [sic!] selects to bear him safely over the ocean's vast bosom he will find here with the acme of perfection.

Approaching the Irish coast, the *Titanic* flew its red and white signal flag – the colours vertical to signify the letter, G – to convey the captain's message: 'I want a pilot.' Not far from the Daunt lightship, off Roche's Point, the pilot came on board. The special pilot for the *Titanic* was John Whelan, aged 57. A friend of his, David Aherne, Cobh's eldest surviving pilot – and himself a 'Cape Horner' because he rounded Cape Horn under sail – told me recently what was involved.

Twelve hours before the estimated time of arrival, John Whelan would have left Queenstown to take up his position in the pilots' signal tower above Roche's Point lighthouse. On sighting the *Titanic* through the telescope he would have ordered his four-man pilot's boat, a former whaler, to put to sea. The oarsmen would have rowed between one-and-a-half and two miles to meet the liner which by then would have slowed to rowing speed. The front oarsman grabbed a rope thrown over the liner's side, allowing the pilot time to jump on to the rope-ladder (known as the Jacob's Ladder) which had been lowered for his arrival.

John Whelan went straight to the bridge and stood beside Captain Edward Smith who was 'in charge of the vessel at all times'. Using his local knowledge, the pilot would have instructed the Captain to follow a straight line-of-sight between the centre of the harbour's mouth and Bennett's Court, a prominent landmark on Great Island in the harbour. A terrace of coastguard houses stood on the mainland to the rear of Roche's Point. As soon as the first of these came into view, Mr. Whelan would have told Edward Smith to drop anchor because this was the spot where the *Titanic* would have 1,000 yards of leeway in any direction.

As soon as the *Titanic* came to a standstill, the two tenders, *Ireland* and *America*, came alongside, one carrying passengers and mail, the other bringing the press reporters and photographers as well as some guests, including Frank's brother, Rev. William Browne.

While Frank Browne was getting his belongings together and taking a few last photographs, three first-class passengers, twenty-seven second-class passengers and one hundred and thirteen steerage passengers came aboard. Recent books have stated that no first-class passengers boarded at Queenstown. Three did. They were Miss Daisy Minahan of Green Bay, Wisconsin, and Dr. and Mrs. William Minahan of Fond du Lac, Winconsin. The two women would survive.

Mr. Thomas Barker, *The Cork Examiner* photographer, knew Frank Browne well and it is likely that they met on board and took pictures together. As we saw in the previous chapter, it was with a *Cork Examiner* photograph that the *Belvederian* article opened.

The *Cork Examiner* reporter who climbed on board was overwhelmed with the beauty of the *Titanic* and in the following day's newspaper devoted two full columns to describing the magnificence of its appointments. Following this, he turned to the question of safety:

> Safety is the first consideration with all voyagers and no excellence can compensate for the lack of it. *Titanic* is the last

word in this respect, double bottom and watertight compartments, steel decks, massive steel plates all in their way making for security, safety and strength. Nothing is left to chance: every mechanical device that could be conceived has been employed to further secure immunity from risk either by sinking or by fire. Should disaster overtake her through contact with rock, instant means can be taken to avert the consequences by concentrating attention on the compartment damaged, which is instantaneously ascertained by an indicator in view of the officer in charge of the bridge who is enabled at the same time by the moving of a lever to close up and seal all or any of the watertight compartments into which the ship is divided. The dangers of the sea, therefore, are practically non-existent on this latest magnificent vessel.

Through the courtesy of Messrs. J. W. Scott & Co., the local agents, a number of Pressmen and others were yesterday shown through the *Titanic* and the arrangements made for the transfer of the mails and passengers in the hands of the firm were of their usual satisfactory character.

The *Titanic* weighed anchor at 1.55 p.m. and proceeded on her first western journey. To the battle of the transatlantic passenger service, the *Titanic* adds a new and important factor of value to the aristocracy and plutocracy attracted from East to West and from West to East. With the *Mauretania* and *Lusitania* of Cunard, the *Olympic* and *Titanic* of the White Star, the *Imperator* and *Kronprinzessin Cecilie* of the Hamburg-Amerika, in the fight during the coming season, there will be a scent of battle all the way from New York to the shores of this country: a contest of sea giants in which the *Titanic* will doubtless take high honours.

At 1.55 p.m., therefore, the liner weighed anchor and the disembarked passengers on the tender, Frank Browne among them, waved good-bye. On moving away the *Titanic* gave the customary three long blasts on her siren to which the tender's hooter replied at similar length. Then the liner gave a final very short blast which was answered in like manner: a single note to bid a final farewell to the ship's company. For most of them it would be very final.

Roche's Point, Cork Harbour, at the spot where the Titanic *dropped anchor.*

The Odell family on board the tender Ireland *after they had disembarked from the* Titanic *with Frank Browne. Young Jack Odell – in school cap – is accompanied by his mother (in lee of wheelhouse). Captain McVeigh stands on the right.*

Another shot on the tender Ireland *in Cork Harbour, showing the writer, R. W. May (centre), standing just behind his brother, Stanley May.*

The photograph here, taken on the boat deck of the Titanic *while at anchor in Cork Harbour, was sent by Father Browne to the* Daily Express *in 1932, so one presumes that he took it himself. He may have been standing beside his friend, Thomas Barker (the* Cork Examiner *photographer) who took similar pictures on the boat deck (see page 112).*

PASSENGERS on the second-class promenade deck.

CHAPTER SEVEN

After the Tragedy

The *Titanic* sank at 2.20 a.m. on the morning of 15th April, 1912. Back in Dublin, Frank Browne's initial reaction to the news was one of relief. As in Montreal, New York and Boston, the Dublin evening newspapers carried a very inaccurate version of the story. The headlines in *The Evening Telegraph* ran:

Terrible Disaster in Mid-Atlantic
Ill-fated Maiden Voyage
Collision with an Iceberg
Women Taken Off by Lifeboats
All the Passengers Saved
***Titanic* on Her Way to Halifax**

The smaller print in that newspaper reported on the reaction to this news at Dublin Port:

> Dublin shipping, which acts as a very generous 'feeder' to the transatlantic liners, was deeply concerned today as to the possible safety of the *Titanic*. Newspapers were grabbed on sight. Telephones and telegraphs were kept busy as each firm concerned begged for the latest intelligence regarding the catastrophe. The possibilities of a rescue formed the sole topic of conversation at Dublin Port today.

Frank would have been more reassured by next morning's Dublin newspapers. *The Irish Times*, for example, read:

The Lost *Titanic*
***Titanic* Sunk**
Disaster To Liner On Maiden Voyage
Struck An Iceberg

The *Titanic* was so seriously damaged that the passengers – over 1470 in number – were at once transferred to the *Parisian* and the *Carpathia*. Fortunately the sea was calm and the operation was safely completed early yesterday morning.

The *Virginian* then took the liner in tow and attempted to get her to Halifax or to the beach near Cape Race. The liner, however, had been too severely damaged to keep afloat and she sank at 2.20 (American Time) yesterday morning.

Following a transcript of the brief Reuter's telegram which simply said: 'New York: the *Titanic* sank at 2.20 this morning', all the Dublin newspapers carried the following bulletin:

> The following statement has been given out by White Star officials:
>
> Captain Haddock of the *Olympic* sends a wireless message that the *Titanic* sank at 2.20 this morning after passengers and crew had been lowered into lifeboats and transferred to the *Virginian*.

All the newspapers, in Ireland as in England, were happy to announce that at Godalming, Surrey, the father of *Titanic's* Marconi operator, Jack Phillips, had received the following message from his son:

> 'Making slowly for Halifax. Practically unsinkable. Don't worry.'

On 16th April, *The Irish Times* was still reassuring:

News Creates Sensation At Queenstown
143 Irish Passengers On Board

The first report circulated, stating that the *Titanic* had foundered as the result of a collision with an iceberg, caused consternation here in Queenstown as 143 passengers had embarked at this port.

The agents of the White Star Company, Messrs. Scott & Co., were happily in a position to reply that the passengers were all safely transferred to the *Virginian*.

It was not until the following day, Wednesday 17th April, that Frank Browne, along with the rest of Ireland, learned the true story. The headlines of *The Irish Times* made heart-breaking reading:

***Titanic* Disaster**
1490 Lives Lost; 868 Survivors
No Passengers On The *Virginian*

Among the pages of coverage, the reader learned that:

> There is now, unhappily, no doubt that the disaster to the *Titanic* is one of the most appalling catastrophes in maritime history. It would appear that the number who have perished reaches the awful figure

DAILY SKETCH.

No. 970.—THURSDAY, APRIL 18, 1912.　　THE PREMIER PICTURE PAPER.　　[Registered as a Newspaper.]　ONE HALFPENNY.

FIRST UNCLOUDED HOURS OF TITANIC'S FATAL VOYAGE.

"Most Remarkable photo ever taken"

We have received from a gentleman who sailed on the Titanic from Southampton last Wednesday and landed at Queenstown on Thursday a series of exclusive photographs he secured on the trip, which have a pathetic interest in view of the terrible fate which awaited the great liner and those on board less than four days after our contributor came ashore at Queenstown. In the first photograph a little boy (probably one of those subsequently dropped into the open boats in the middle of the night and at this moment being carried to New York on board the Carpathia) is seen spinning his top on the saloon deck on Thursday morning, whilst men, now buried in the Atlantic, look on. The second snapshot was seen under the bridge as the Titanic steamed out to sea down the Solent.

102

of 1490. [In fact over 1500 people lost their lives.] The terrible calamity has caused the greatest consternation throughout the world.

St. John's, Newfoundland, Tuesday: All hope of any passengers or members of the crew of the *Titanic*, other than those on board the *Carpathia*, being alive has now been abandoned and this afternoon all steamers which had been cruising in the vicinity of the disaster continued their voyages.

Queenstown, Tuesday: It would be impossible to describe the dismay with which news of the terrible catastrophe to the *Titanic* and her freight of human souls was received here this morning.

People arrived here this afternoon from various parts of the country and it was distressing to see the great anxiety with which they endeavoured to get news of some helpful kind from the White Star offices.

On the same day, the Dublin *Evening Telegraph* unravelled the mystery of that telegram from Marconi-man Phillips:

Mistake About A Message

The Press Association, Godalming correspondent, telegraphs:

The message stated to have been received last night by Mr. & Mrs. Phillips from their son, the wireless operator aboard the *Titanic*, turns out not to have been from him at all, but from another son in London. On receiving the message the father came to the conclusion that it was from his son on the *Titanic*, but this morning he stated that he must have been mistaken.

Frank Browne must have been shattered to read this news because he had chatted with Jack Phillips at least twice. They had met on board the *Adriatic* as well as in the Marconi Room of the *Titanic*.

Frank Browne kept no record of his photographic sales at the time, but we know that his pictures appeared in newspapers across the globe, a British 'exclusive' being given to London's *Daily Sketch*.

Facing and below: Two photographs which Father Browne took of London's Daily Sketch, *18 April, 1912. His handwritten note on the facing photograph is explained in chapter eight.*

On 19th April, he travelled from Dublin to Queenstown where he photographed the town in mourning and showed the White Star flag at half-staff. The Cunard flag was similarly flying in sympathy.

On 22nd April, he attended the Requiem Mass at St. Colman's Cathedral, Queenstown. Bishop Robert Browne officiated and the cathedral was packed to capacity.

In the light of the terrible catastrophe, naturally, every little memento of the *Titanic* became precious. The card given to him by the liner's physical education officer, for example, acquired a tragic proportion when Frank Browne learned that the friendly gymnast had lost his life.

The passengers who had disembarked together at Queenstown began to correspond with one another. Frank kept the letters he was sent at this time as well as the *Titanic* menu card which somebody conveyed to him by post. It was assigned to an envelope marked 'Very Important'.

Queenstown in mourning, with flags at half-staff, 19 April, 1912. The building on the left is the Cunard Office, now Trustee Savings Bank, with the White Star agents, Messrs James Scott & Company, to the rear. The tenders Ireland *and* America *can be seen moored to the right. The deserted quay tells its own story.*

The SS Titanic called at Queenstown on Thursday 11th April, 1912
and embarked Mails and Passengers for New York on her Maiden Voyage.
Passengers and Crew, 2,358.

At a Meeting of the Board held on Wednesday 17th April 1912, Mr. C. J. Engledew in very feeling language referred to the very appalling disaster to the White Star Steamship Titanic, *which Vessel struck an Iceberg, off the banks of Newfoundland, and was lost in latitude 41-46 North and Longitude 50-14 West on the morning of the 15th instant and which calamity swamped in death over 1,600 persons.*

The catastrophe he described as the most terrible in the history of the Sea, and moved the following resolution which he suggested should be transmitted to Messrs Ismay Imrie & Co. through Mr. J. W. Scott (Queenstown) Agent, White Star Line:

That we the Members of the Cork Harbour Board desire to convey to the friends and relatives of those who have lost their lives in the Titanic *disaster, and also to Messrs Ismay Imrie & Co. our deepest and most sincere sympathy with them in the dreadful loss that has overtaken them.*

Mr. Haughton also in sympathetic language seconded the motion which was supported by several Members and put by the Chairman and unanimously agreed to.

From Father Browne's Titanic Album *–
a cherished memento given to Frank Browne by
Mr. McCawley, the liner's physical education officer,
who lost his life in the tragedy.*

EXCESSIVE SPEED
What the Californian might have done.

Lord Mersey yesterday delivered the judgment of the Court that inquired into the loss of the *Titanic*.

Many ladies went to the Scottish Hall, Buckingham Gate, to hear the judgment read, among them an elderly woman in mourning, her hat trimmed with ostrich feathers.

Lord Mersey found that the disaster was due to collision with an iceberg brought about by the excessive speed at which the ship was being navigated. Captain Smith made a very grievous mistake in not reducing speed at night when he reached the region where ice might be expected; but in view of the fact that it had not been the practice of liners to reduce speed so long as the weather was clear he was not guilty of negligence and it was impossible to fix him with blame.

It was to be hoped that the last had been heard of the practice of going at full speed at night in an ice region – a practice due probably to competition and the desire of the public for quick passages.

It was irregular for Captain Smith to give Mr Ismay the *Baltic's* ice message and improper for Mr Ismay to retain it, but that incident had no influence on navigation.

Lord Mersey did not believe that the presence of Mr Ismay on board induced Captain Smith to neglect precautions that he would otherwise have taken; Captain Smith was not trying to please anybody, but was exercising his own discretion.

SIR COSMO DUFF-GORDON.
The ladies took a keen interest in that part of the judgment dealing with Sir Cosmo Duff-Gordon. It will be remembered that the calling of Sir Cosmo and Lady Duff-Gordon as witnesses attracted large numbers of women to the inquiry. Lord Mersey found that the gross charge made against Sir Cosmo of having bribed the crew of No.1 boat to row away from the drowning people was unfounded.

Lord Mersey did not agree that Mr. Bruce Ismay's position as managing director of the company imposed on him a moral duty to wait on board until the ship sank. If he had not jumped into the boat another life would have been lost.

As for the *Californian*, the Court's finding was that when she first saw the rockets the *Californian* could have pushed through the ice to the open water without any serious risk and so have come to the assistance of the *Titanic*. Had she done so, she might have saved many, if not all of the lives that were lost.

A good and proper look-out for ice was not kept. An extra look-out should have been placed on the stem-head and a sharp look-out from both sides of the bridge.

Frank Browne followed the Titanic *investigation avidly in the newspapers and kept many press cuttings such as this. From his correspondence we know that he was inclined to agree with the investigators' findings, in general, though he disagreed with the suggestion – and could prove this from his photographs – that Captain Smith was aiming for record time. As for the* Californian, *we now know she was further away than the investigators thought and could have saved nobody*

Frank Browne collated all the letters he received from fellow-passengers on the *Titanic*, some of whom wrote frequently. I have selected a few reproduced here that convey their content.

18 April, 1912

Dear Father Browne,
    We only heard yesterday of the awful news of the shipwreck of the Titanic. *It is all most terribly sad and I can hardly realise that that enormous mass of ironwork is at the bottom of the ocean and such a fearful loss of life. I wonder if any of your friends escaped?*
    . . . Now your photos will have a sad interest in them . . .
    Thanks for all your kindness to us on board the ill-fated Titanic.
    Yours sincerely,
    G. T. Noel,
    Finisterre,
    France.

20 April, 1912

Dear Friend,
    We feel that we must write to you as we were all passengers on the poor Titanic *together. What an awful disaster it is. We have wondered so much whether the gentleman friend of the lady who came ashore with us at Queenstown is saved, as we do not know his name. If you know it, will you kindly let us have it . . .*
    With kind regards,
    Yours sincerely,
    (Mrs) L. Odell,
    Stile House, Lyme Regis,
    Dorset.

20 May, 1912

My dear Father Browne,
    I do not know how to thank you sufficiently for your great kindness in sending such a splendid lot of photos which are of great interest – rather melancholy interest.
    If you are ever in this part of the country, do let us know, as we should all be so pleased to see you here.
    Yours sincerely
    G. T. Noel,
    Temple Guiting House,
    Winchcombe,
    Glos.

The most voluminous correspondence was with the writer, R.W. May, brother of Mrs. Odell, and therefore an uncle of the Jack Odell whose picture we have seen on page 58. His first letter was oddly addressed, as shown above.

20 April, 1912

My dear Sir,

I hope this queerly addressed letter will reach you. You will doubtless remember us all sitting together on the ill-fated Titanic *so I take the liberty 1st of asking you if you would favour me with some copies of your excellent photos some of which I've seen printed, one of which has my little nephew. 2ndly, do you happen to know the names of the lady and gentleman at your left at table and whether they are among the saved?*

Yours faithfully,
R. W. May,
Gresham Road, Brixton, S.W.

8 May, 1912

My dear Sir,

Accept my best thanks for your very kind letter. I shall look forward to my copies of the photos you can send me. When I get some of those we took, I'll be prepared to let you have a few. Perhaps my sister, Mrs. Odell, has already promised them to you . . .

I return the "W. S. Co" lecture to you. The lady's name was, I believe, Mrs Noden. The gentleman's name I did not have at all, so cannot say if among the saved or not. I was so glad to hear you had a prize for your pictures. *

Yours truly,
R. W. May.

4 May, 1912

Dear Mr Browne,

Very many thanks . . . Have you ever heard of this little book and will you accept it with my thanks for what you so kindly did for me.

Yours sincerely,
R. W. May.

17 June, 1912

Dear Mr Browne,

Many thanks for The Belvederian *containing your excellent article, I've taken the liberty of writing to Dublin and asking for three copies to be sent to me . . . The allusions to Mr. McElroy and Mr Nicholson are aptly appropriate and just enough.*

I suppose you are following the Enquiry. In places I think a little levity is shown. A pity, but time I suppose as usual tends to assuage the grief of loss. But a moment's reflection, on my part, brings everything so vividly to mind. One cannot think of any part of the occurence light-heartedly.

Another book is approaching completion. I hope to send you a copy shortly.

Sincerely yours,
R. W. May.

1 January, 1913

Dear Mr Browne,

Accept my best wishes to you for 1913, though a little late. I never wrote and thanked you for the last photo. I think it's indeed quite a curio and I like it even better than the one with poor Smith looking down from the bridge. You said you had the negative . . .

Sincerely yours,
R. W. May.

*This is the only reference I could find for Frank Browne having won a prize for his *Titanic* photographs.

107

Requiem Mass in St. Colman's Cathedral, Queenstown, on 22 April, 1912. The photographer's uncle, Bishop Robert Browne, presided.

CHAPTER EIGHT

In Later Years

Early in 1913 Frank Browne started to give public lectures on the *Titanic*, illustrated with lantern slides. To supplement his own *Titanic* photographs he acquired materials that dealt with the disaster itself such as the ships' radio messages and illustrations from a variety of sources of the actual sinking.

Obviously, the White Star Line heard about the Browne lectures because in March 1913 the letter reproduced on page 110 reached Frank Browne in Dublin. 'We shall be glad' it announces, 'to obtain photographs of the illustrations to which you allude in the "Olympic" booklet,' and then continues with a truly breathtaking request, 'but shall appreciate it if in any lectures you deliver, you will abstain from any reference to the "Titanic", as you will understand that we do not wish the memory of this calamity should be perpetuated.'

As every schoolgirl and schoolboy knows, the reason so many lives were lost at the time of the disaster was that the *Titanic* did not have enough lifeboats. As a result of the investigation, ships were thenceforth required to carry sufficient lifeboat capacity for everyone on board. The photographs on pages 114 and 115 show how this edict was put into practice.

The *Daily Express* of London commemorated the twentieth anniversary of the loss of the *Titanic* on the 15th April, 1932 and it used Father Browne's photographs to illustrate the text. Its front page is reproduced here as is the 1937 newspaper feature about that wonderful but untrue tale of 'The Most Romantic Picture Ever Taken'. This was in the edition marking the twenty-fifth anniversary of the catastrophe, of the *Weekly Illustrated* of London which also used the Browne photographs.

Father Browne, in fact, did not know that his photograph 'The Children's Playground' (see page 66) showed the Spedden boy. He was definitely of the opinion that the boy spinning his top on the Saloon Deck was one of the famous 'Titanic Orphans' who were about to be adopted by Mrs Guggenheim when their true identity emerged. He believed this to be one of the French boys whose father had taken them aboard *Titanic* without their mother's knowledge.

The *Weekly Illustrated* feature quotes Father Browne as saying that the boy's mother saw this photograph of one of her sons in a Spanish newspaper and was able to travel to New York and reclaim her sons, and indeed in 1937, Father Browne was still under the impression that it was his photograph that the mother had seen. With hindsight, we know that it must have been one of the American wire pictures which had appeared in that Spanish newspaper. Somebody, confusing these photographs, obviously told the priest that his photography had worked a wonder: he was not a man to invent such a fantasy himself.

White Star letter sent to Frank Browne on 4 March, 1913

I, COCKSPUR STREET, S.W.
"Oceanic House".
38, LEADENHALL STREET, E.C.
LONDON.

CANUTE ROAD, SOUTHAMPTON.
9, BROADWAY, NEW YORK.
84, STATE ST. BOSTON.
118, NOTRE DAME ST WEST, MONTREAL.
53, DALHOUSIE ST QUEBEC.
21, PIAZZA DELLA BORSA, NAPLES.
VIA ALLA NUNZIATA, Nº 18, GENOA.
PARIS AGENT: NICHOLAS MARTIN, 9, RUE SCRIBE.
30, JAMES ST, LIVERPOOL.
TELEGRAPHIC ADDRESS "OCEANIC, LIVERPOOL".

McC.
S.

Advertising   DEPARTMENT.

(PLEASE ADDRESS ANY REPLY TO THE MANAGERS & MENTION THE DEPARTMENT.)

LIVERPOOL,   March 4th, 1913.

The Rev: F.M.Brown, S.J.
Milltown Park,
DUBLIN.

WHITE STAR LINE SERVICES.

SOUTHAMPTON–CHERBOURG–NEW YORK.
ROYAL & UNITED STATES MAIL STEAMERS.
VIA QUEENSTOWN (WESTBOUND)–PLYMOUTH (EASTBOUND)

LIVERPOOL–NEW YORK.
VIA QUEENSTOWN.

LIVERPOOL–NEW YORK.
(FREIGHT.)

LIVERPOOL–BOSTON.
VIA QUEENSTOWN.

LIVERPOOL–QUEBEC–MONTREAL.
LIVERPOOL–HALIFAX–PORTLAND.

LIVERPOOL–AUSTRALIA.
VIA SOUTH AFRICA.

LIVERPOOL–AUSTRALIA.
(FREIGHT.)

LIVERPOOL–NEW ZEALAND.
(FREIGHT.)

LONDON–NEW ZEALAND.
VIA SOUTH AFRICA.

NEW YORK–MEDITERRANEAN.
VIA AZORES.

BOSTON–MEDITERRANEAN.
VIA AZORES.

THROUGH BOOKINGS
TO ALL PARTS
OF THE WORLD.

Dear Sir,

We duly received your favour of the 1st instant, all contents of which have our careful attention.

We shall be glad to obtain photographs of the illustrations to which you allude in the "Olympic" booklet, but shall appreciate it if in any lectures you deliver, you will abstain from any reference to the loss of the "Titanic", as you will easily understand that we do not wish the memory of this calamity should be perpetuated.

Yours faithfully,

For WHITE STAR LINE.

Right: *An illustration of the* Titanic *at night, anchored off Cherbourg. This was used by Frank Browne for his public lectures and was taken from the supplement to* The Sphere, *London, 20th April, 1912.*

Below: *The* Titanic *sinks. Artist's impression from the same issue of* The Sphere. *This was turned into a lantern-slide and used (with permission) by Frank Browne in his public lectures.*

On the front cover, the London *Weekly Illustrated* of 10 April, 1912, described one of Father Browne's photographs as 'the most romantic picture ever taken'. This referred to the photograph of Douglas Spedden (see page 66). The inside feature, shown here, elaborates.

Father Browne, in fact, did not know that this photograph showed the Spedden boy. He was definitely of the opinion that the boy spinning his top on the Saloon Deck was one of the famous '*Titanic* Orphans' who were about to be adopted by Mrs. Guggenheim when their true identity emerged.

As Father Browne heard it, M. Navratil, a rich man living in the south of France, decided in April 1912 to abscond with his children's governess. Hiring a car under an assumed name, the couple drove to Cherbourg with the man's two sons who were then aged four years and two years respectively. The four sailed on the *Titanic* and, after the collision with the iceberg, the boys were given space in a lifeboat and were eventually rescued by the *Carpathia*. Both the governess and M. Navratil were lost.

The *Weekly Illustrated* of 1937 quotes Father Browne as saying that the boys' mother saw 'this photograph of mine' in a Spanish newspaper – the picture entitled 'The Children's Playground' – and was able to travel to New York and reclaim her sons.

In 1937, Frank Browne was still under the impression that it was his photograph that the mother had seen. With hindsight we know that it must have been one of the American wire pictures which appeared in that Spanish newspaper. Somebody, confusing the photographs, obviously told the priest that his photograph had worked a wonder: he was not a man to invent such a story.

Facing page: *The front page of London's* Daily Express, *15 April, 1932*

Above: *After the* Titanic *disaster, all ships had to carry sufficient lifeboats to save all on board. Here we see 'Berthon' collapsible boats on board the White Star liner* Majestic.

Left: *Extra lifeboats were placed on the decks on the White Star liner* Baltic *to implement the new British Board of Trade ruling.*

'Henderson' collapsible boats on the White Star liner Arabic. Besides the solid gunwales, the keels of these boats are also solid. On being lifted up, they open like a concertina and are then kept in shape by means of struts and bolts. They could accommodate about twenty people.

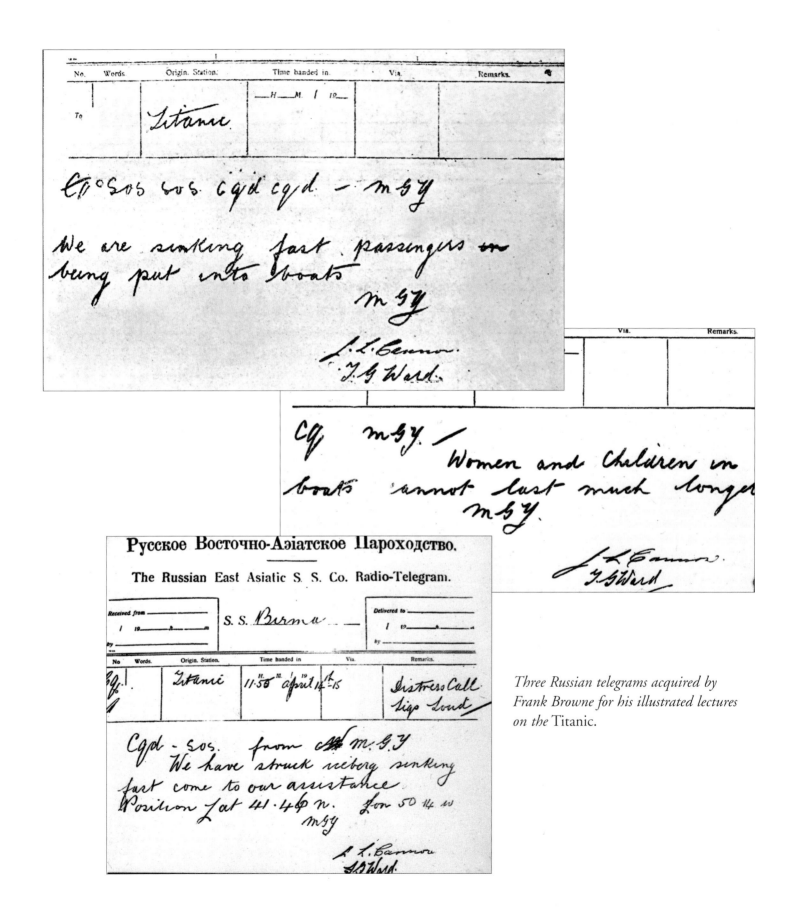

No.	Words	Origin. Station.	Time handed in.		Via.	Remarks.
To		Titanic	— H — M / 19			

CQ° SOS SOS. CQD CQD — MGY

We are sinking fast passengers are
being put into boats
M GY

S. L. Cennor.
T. G Ward.

			Via.	Remarks.

CQ MGY /

boats cannot last much longer

Women and Children in

MGY.

S. L. Cennor.
T. G Ward

Русское Восточно-Азіатское Пароходство.

The Russian East Asiatic S. S. Co. Radio-Telegram.

Received from ____	S. S. Birma	Delivered to ____
/ 19 ___ h ___ m		/ 19 ___ h ___
by ____		by ____

No	Words.	Origin. Station.	Time handed in	Via.	Remarks.
		Titanic	11·55 M / 19 April 14th 15		Distress Call Sigs Loud

Cqd — sos. from M.G.Y
We have struck iceberg sinking
fast come to our assistance
Position Lat 41·46 N. Lon 50 14 W
MGY

S. L. Cennor
T.G Ward.

*Three Russian telegrams acquired by
Frank Browne for his illustrated lectures
on the* Titanic.

CHAPTER NINE

In Memoriam

This final photograph catches well the mood of the poem (shown overleaf) written by Father Browne shortly after the ship sank. It shows the *Titanic* Memorial in Donegall Square, Belfast, taken by Father Browne in 1937.

The picture, with its ironic back-drop of the Ocean Accident & Guarantee Company, could not be taken nowadays because the statue was moved to a different side of Donegall Square some years ago.

'IN MEMORIAM'
April 15th, 1912

'As a ship that passeth through the waves, whereof when it is gone by, the trace cannot be found, nor the path of its keel in the waters.' Wisdom, 5:10.

A Ship rode forth on the Noonday tide
    Rode forth to the open sea,
And the high sun shone on the good ship's side,
And all seemed gladness, and hope, and pride
    For a gallant sight was she.

For the crew was strong, and the captain brave
    And never a fear had they,
Never a thought for the turbulent wave,
Never a dread of a watery grave,
    Nor dreams of a fateful day.

So the ship sailed on, and the voices strong
    Sang sweet on the morning air,
And the glad notes billowed the shore along,
Then drifted and died, till the Sailors' song
    Was soft as a whispered prayer.

And all seemed gladness, and hope, and pride,
    As far as the eye could see,
For where was the foe that could pierce her side,
Or where in the Ocean depths could hide,
    A mightier power than she?

But far to the North, in the frozen zone
    Where the Ice King holds his sway,
Full many a berg, like a monarch's throne,
Or castle that fabled princes own
    Gleamed white neath the Sun's bright ray.

When the challenge came on the whisp'ring air
    It passed like a fleeting breath,
But it roused the King in his Arctic lair,
And waked what vengeance was sleeping there,
    The vengeance of Doom and Death.

But heedless and gay o'er the sunlit waves
    The vessel all lightly bore,
Till the distant coast with its rocks and caves,
And the land that the Western Ocean laves,
    Were seen from her decks no more.

When Evening came with its waning light,
    And shrouded the rolling deep,
For never a moment she stayed her flight,
Adown the path of the moonbeams bright,
    Though Heaven was wrapped in sleep.

Another dawn with its liquid gold
    Gilded the Eastern sky
Lighting the Ship so fair, so bold,
That sped its way o'er the Ocean old,
    Nor recked of danger nigh....

And noonday came, when the burning sun
    Rifted the realms of snow,
And burst the fetters the Ice had spun
And shattered the towers that Cold had won,
    Breaking the great Ice-flow.

Till over the ocean's heaving swell,
    Like ghosts in the twilight gloom,
The great bergs glided with purpose fell
Minding the quest of their Monarch well,
    The quest of Revenge and Doom.

The deeper night with its slow advance
    Bids even the winds to cease,
No moonbeams bright on the waters dance
But all lies still in a starry trance
    And the Ocean sleeps in peace.

A shuddering gasp o'er the resting deep!
    A wail from the silent sea!
Tis heard where the stars their lone watch keep
Tis heard in the graves where dead men sleep,
    mindful of human glee . . .

The Springtime dawn with its rosy light
    Sees naught but the waves' wild flow
For under the veil of the moonless night
When the sea was still and the stars were bright
    The Ice King had slain his foe.

The Ship that rode on noonday tide
    Rode forth to the open sea,
But gone are the gladness, and hope and pride,
For the Northern Ocean's depths could hide,
    A mightier power than she.

The Ship that rode on noonday tide
*   Rode forth to the open sea,*
But gone are her gladness, hope, & pride,
For the Northern Ocean's depths could hide,
*   A mightier power than she.*

118

| 1908 | White Star Line signs contract with Harland & Wolff, Belfast shipbuilders, for three new liners, *Olympic*, *Titanic* and *Gigantic*. Construction of *Olympic* begins. |

1909 — Construction of *Titanic* begins.

1910 — *Olympic* launched.

1911 — *Titanic* launched.
Maiden voyage of *Olympic*.

1912 — Construction of *Gigantic* begins (Her name will be changed to *Britannic* after the April tragedy).

March — Fitting out of *Titanic* completed. Modifications and improvements will make her heavier than *Olympic*, and thus the largest ship afloat.
Specifications:
  Length: 882 feet 9 inches.
  Breadth: 94 feet.
  Height: 180 feet (including funnels which rise 84 feet above Boat Deck).
  Engines: 46,000 horsepower.
  Capacity: 46,328 tons.
  Displacement: 52,250 tons.

2 April — Sea trials in the Irish Sea. *Titanic* reaches a speed of 20 knots (although capable of 24 knots).

3 April — *Titanic* reaches Southampton where provisioning and staffing begin.

10 April — Frank Browne travels by train from London to Southampton.
Maiden voyage of *Titanic* begins under Captain Edward Smith, formerly Captain of *Olympic*.
Titanic reaches Cherbourg, France at 6.30 p.m.

11 April — Voyage from Cherbourg to Queenstown (Cobh), Ireland, where Frank Browne disembarks.
Titanic sails for New York at 1.55 p.m.

14 April — *Titanic* collides with iceberg at 11.40 p.m.
Stated position (see page 116) 40° 46′ N, 50° 14′ W.
Actual position (13.5 miles away) 41° 44′ N, 49° 57′ W.
Conditions: 'Flat Calm'.
Sky: Cloudless.
Temperature: 31° F (-1° C).

15 April — 12.25 a.m. Passengers told to take to the lifeboats, 'women and children first'.
Board of Trade Lifeboat Requirement: 962 spaces (for a maximum total of 3,511 passengers and crew.).

Titanic's Lifeboat Capacity (16 lifeboats, plus four collapsible boats): 1,178 spaces (for an approximate total of 2,225 passengers and crew at the time).
2.20 a.m. *Titanic* sinks.
  Approx. 1,520 passengers and crew perish.

4.10 a.m. *Carpathia* reaches scene of the tragedy.

18 April — *Carpathia* reaches New York with 705 survivors, the only ones to be saved; and Frank Browne's photographs appear in newspapers.

19 April — U.S. Senate Investigation into *Titanic* disaster begins. It will end on 25 May. Its Report will call for the setting up of a commission to investigate all laws and regulations regarding construction and equipment of ocean-going vessels.

2 May — British Board of Trade Investigation into *Titanic* disaster begins. Its Recommendations, issued on 3 July, will call for the better provision of lifeboats and for more watertight compartments.

1913 — *Olympic* back in service after extensive renovations in Belfast.
Frank Browne gives illustrated lectures on White Star Line.

1914 — *Britannic* launched.

1915 — Frank Browne is ordained a priest on 31 July.

1916 — *Britannic*, now a World War I hospital ship, sunk by German mines off Crete.

1920 — Father Browne compiles *Titanic* album.

1932 — London's *Daily Express* features Father Browne's *Titanic* photographs.

1935 — *Olympic* scrapped after 24 years of transatlantic service.

1937 — London's *Weekly Illustrated* features Father Browne's *Titanic* Photographs.

1985 — Wreck of *Titanic* found at depth of 12,460 feet on expedition led by Dr. Robert D. Ballard of Woods Hole Oceanographic Institute, Massachusetts, USA.
42,000 photographic negatives of Father Browne discovered in Dublin basement by E.E. O'Donnell SJ.

INDEX